PSYCHIATRIC EMERGENCIES

NURSING ASSESSMENT AND INTERVENTION

Sandra Talley
Mary C. King

PSYCHIATRIC EMERGENCIES Nursing Assessment and Intervention

PSYCHIATRIC EMERGENCIES
Nursing Assessment and Intervention

Sandra L. Talley, R.N., M.N., C.S.
Chairperson, Psychiatric-Mental Health
Nursing Program
Yale University School of Nursing

Mary Catherine King, R.N., M.Ed., N.P.
Assistant Professor
Department of Mental Health Nursing
School of Nursing
Oregon Health Sciences University

MACMILLAN PUBLISHING COMPANY
New York

Collier Macmillan Canada, Inc.
TORONTO

Collier Macmillan Publishers
LONDON

Macmillan Publishing Company
866 Third Avenue, New York, New York 10022

Collier Macmillan Canada, Inc.
Collier Macmillan Publishers • London

Library of Congress Cataloging in Publication Data

Talley, Sandra L.
  Psychiatric emergencies.

  Includes bibliographies and index.
    1. Crisis intervention (Psychiatry)—Handbooks,
manuals, etc.   2. Psychiatric emergencies—Handbooks,
manuals, etc.   3. Psychiatric nursing—Handbooks,
manuals, etc.   I. King, Mary Catherine.   II. Title.
[DNLM: 1. Crisis Intervention.   2. Emergencies.
3. Psychiatric Nursing.   WY 160 T148p]
RC480.6.T35   1984   616.89'025   84-21797
ISBN 0-02-418800-X

Printing: 1 2 3 4 5 6 7 8   Year: 4 5 6 7 8 9 0 1 2

Dedicated to our students, whose enthusiasm for learning
motivated us to conceptualize our clinical teaching.

Preface

Psychiatric nurses in emergency care attempt to meet clients during a time of immediate need. The goal is to evaluate the problem from both the client's perspective and the nurse's clinical expertise. The nurse develops a plan of care that is clinically sound, attends to the client's perceived needs, and effectively utilizes available resources. Often the emergency situation is further complicated by elements of suicidal or homicidal risk, making swift and accurate decision making even more crucial. Common denominators for this type of nursing care are confidence, empathy, knowledge, and the ability to engage the client in a systematic approach to problem solving. This book is intended to offer a practical framework to help nurses mobilize these skills when faced with psychiatric emergencies.

As educators in clinical settings, the authors have each mastered individual styles of assignment and identified similar components as essential to the assessment process. However, the translation of clinical experience into educational principles requires an organizational framework to simplify the learning experience. It is tempting to label experienced clinical judgements as *intuitive* processes rather than identifying their roots in formal knowledge bases. In an effort to make the translation from clincial experience to educational guidance, the authors devised a decision-making framework for graduate students in psychiatric-mental health nursing who were placed in the emergency service.

The knowledge base most applicable to psychiatric emergency services was derived from psychiatric, sociological, and nursing processes. The emphasis is on assessment of the clinical problem, evaluation of the risk in the immediate situation, and implementation of treatment plans that are acceptable to clients and available in the community. This book has been organized around these three areas.

Chapters 2 and 3 (Assessment of the Clinical Problem and Decision Making in Clinical Assessment, respectively) review the standard content necessary to assess the client's complaints. Examples include the mental status examination, the psychiatric history, and a medical evaluation. This material is then woven into a decision-making model that guides the clinician toward general diagnostic categories. Lastly, the clinical findings for each diagnostic category are compared and contrasted to give the reader a *picture* of clients with different clinical problems. Explanations for different types of data are based on psychopathological dysfunctions, sociocultural differences, and occupational/financial/personal resources.

In addition to assessment of the clinical problem, the clinician must determine the risk inherent in each situation. Chapters 4 and 5 review assessment of suicide and dangerousness, respectively. Scales for suicide assessment are included, as well as a discussion of factors related to dangerous behavior in psychiatric clients.

Once the nurse has evaluated the clinical problem and the degree of risk, treatment interventions can follow. The discussion on treatment planning includes the client's perspective in using health care resources with the hope of improving adherence to the treatment plan. Chapters 6, 7, and 8 discuss these concepts of enabling factors and adherence to treatment recommendations.

The remaining Chapters, 9 and 10, provide an overview of psychiatric emergency services, and the future potential of emergency care models.

This book has been written for nurses who practice in expanded roles such as the psychiatric emergency service. Many of the health care principles used in this setting are not unique to nursing, but rather complement the psychiatric nursing perspective. A major thread throughout the text is client-centered care with an emphasis on sound clinical decision making and judicious use of mental health care resources. It is our belief that nurses can become expert in the assessment of psychiatric emergency situations and merge this expertise with their client advocacy role in planning safe, acceptable interventions.

The authors' enthusiasm for the nurse's role in psychiatric emergency services is based on the degree of autonomy inherent in this practice arena, and the opportunities to negotiate treatment plans that are clinically sound and accommodate the client's individual needs for care. The selection of the clinical content included in this book was based on the assumption that assessment and care planning must be clinically and theoretically sound, yet these are effective only when they have attended to the client's perspective and perceived need for care. To facilitate mastery of this approach, the content has been organized into steps which take the reader through the problem-solving process for a multitude of clinical situations.

Attention to the *process* of assessment and intervention planning will hopefully encourage nurses to broadly view each situation and assign clinically significant hypotheses to the information gathered. This open-minded approach prevents early closure on assessment and balances the strengths and weaknesses in each client's life context.

We would like to thank several individuals at our respective institutions for their contribution in the completion of this project. Pam Warner, Secretary, Yale University School of Nursing, for her willingness to type several manuscripts under the pressure of deadlines; Dolores Leona, Staff Assistant, Yale University School of Nursing, who managed many of the program tasks making completion of this project possible and who also offered helpful comments and editorial assistance in the final manuscript; Nora Goicoechea, Head Nurse, Neuropsychiatric Unit, Yale-New Haven Hospital, whose critical comments of drafts helped us maintain our original perspective and reinforced the value of the clinical emphasis in the book; Mary Cowan, Research Assistant, Oregon Health Sciences University, School of Nursing, for her assistance in reviewing the literature for a part of this book; and Lisa Ferris-Leech, Secretary, Oregon Health Sciences University, for her generosity in prioritizing numerous rough drafts. We wish to express our sincere appreciation to each of these individuals.

Contents

PSYCHIATRIC EMERGENCIES
Nursing Assessment and Intervention

PSYCHIATRIC EMERGENCY SERVICES

Since the 1950s, the concept of emergency psychiatric care has become increasingly recognized as an adjunctive method of delivering mental health services.[1] Emergency psychiatric care has evolved into a time-limited form of treatment available to clients who are unable or unwilling to utilize other forms of psychiatric treatment. This model has built on the crisis intervention method by adding in-depth psychiatric assessment, linking clients with secondary treatment resources, and offering brief treatment to clients awaiting admission or outpatient care.

Placement of these psychiatric emergency service programs has been dictated by client demand and availability of trained psychiatric staff. Community mental health centers have set aside staff time to evaluate clients who present for care but have not been assigned a therapist, and general hospital emergency rooms have hired psychiatrists to screen the increasing volume of psychiatric patients who request treatment in that setting. These services initially focused on diagnosing the client's problem and making a referral to another treatment setting.[2]

During the 1970s, research studies radically changed the focus of these programs. First, data showed that the number of clients

3

seeking care through psychiatric emergency services was growing at a rapid rate; secondly, less than half of the referrals made to outpatient programs were completed.[3,4] In spite of the findings of poor follow-up with referrals, clients continued to find the emergency care model attractive. Efforts were subsequently redirected to increase available staff and assist clients in resolving their crises and/or accepting continued care in more suitable community programs.

These additional services have broadened the scope of practice termed *emergency psychiatric care.*[5] Outreach programs have been designed to follow clients more closely after their initial contact in the hope of bringing about problem resolution or stabilization in an outpatient treatment setting. Increasing the number of staff from other disciplines such as nursing and social work has broadened the treatment perspective beyond the medical model of care. Psychiatrists have been utilized more appropriately for diagnosing clients' problems and consulting with staff, while members of other disciplines have arranged for inpatient or outpatient care for clients, facilitated family involvement in caring for clients, and provided direct care through brief therapy techniques.

The *emergency* component of psychiatric care is an additional service in mental health care. It should not be viewed as an extension of either inpatient or outpatient psychiatric programs, but rather as an adjunctive or alternative resource for many clients. As an alternative resource, it offers easily accessible care, access to highly trained psychiatric staff, minimal stigmatization when associated with a general hospital setting, and fewer motivational constraints when requesting care. Currently, there are four major areas of care that comprise emergency services.

1. Preadmission care. Assessment and evaluation of clients who will require additional psychiatric treatment. The emphasis is on discovery of the etiology of the client's problem, the resources necessary to facilitate admission to a suitable setting, and the location of a treatment program.

2. Crisis care. Assessment and treatment of those problems which can be resolved through the emergency service and do not require the assistance of an additional treatment resource.

3. Transition care. Treatment of clients for a brief period of time until a secondary treatment resource is located. This may include acute management of severely disturbed clients in the emergency service holding bed area or return visits for clients who are awaiting an outpatient clinic appointment.

4. Linkage with community resources. Provision of information and/or an appointment with a community resource unknown to

the client. Care is not necessary before the client seeks continued services from another resource.

Psychiatric emergency services are aimed at solving an immediate problem faced by the client and his or her family. This type of service model is not designed to compete with existing programs. Thus, clients with severe mental disorders are referred to appropriate treatment settings, and emergency care is limited to assessment and referral activities. The use of highly trained professional staff ensures that evaluations address both psychiatric and medical etiologies of psychopathological behavior and that referrals place the client into the most appropriate treatment setting. For those clients not interested in or unlikely to enter another treatment setting, staff may deliver brief treatment in an attempt to maximize the emergency contact with psychiatry.

Psychology of Emergency Psychiatric Care

Understanding the attractiveness of emergency psychiatric services is important in structuring the services provided to clients. Any enthusiasm generated by health care providers must be tempered by the long-standing criticisms of these services by psychiatric clinicians. These conflicting goals of clients and clinicians represent the growing discontent with health care in general. Clients demand greater access to services during critical periods in their lives, whereas health professionals require organized health care delivery systems and motivation on the part of clients, as indicated by keeping regularly scheduled appointments, following through with prescribed treatment plans, and so on. The emergency care model allows clients to bypass many of these requirements and arrive for care when it is deemed necessary.

This arrangement leaves the locus of control for mental health care in the hands of the client, without much countercontrol by the clinician. Similarly, because visits to the emergency service are brief, opportunities for long-range behavior change are kept to a minimum. Again, this challenges much of our philosophy about how emotional problems are resolved over time through a client–therapist relationship. In fact, those clients who prefer the structure of an emergency service model may be attracted to an institution-based program rather than a particular therapist. Working through transferences, long-standing themes, and unconscious conflicts is less likely to be the focus of an emergency visit than a regularly scheduled outpatient psychotherapy session. For many clients the emergency visit is less threatening, demands little long-range commitment, yet provides them with an attentive, well-trained professional who will listen to their problems.

The existence of emergency psychiatric service programs need not erode the long-standing values of traditional psychiatric services, nor should these programs be viewed as competitive, alternative treatment modalities. As an additional mental health resource, these programs assist families with an acutely disturbed member to gain access to inpatient psychiatric treatment; they renew medication for clients newly arrived in a city and direct them to outpatient treatment settings; and they counsel distressed individuals who are unable to wait for outpatient psychiatric services that have long waiting lists. Their location in an emergency room setting gives them access to rape victims and survivors of suicide attempts. For some clients, the emergency service becomes their only contact with mental health care secondary to their resistance to treatment, as the following case illustrates.

Clinical Example 1–1

A 25-year-old single white male presented to the emergency room requesting psychiatric care. He complained of feeling controlled by beings from another planet, had not been sleeping well, and had withdrawn from his friends. These delusions were long-standing but usually under better control. The patient was not homicidal or suicidal and had no history of dangerous behavior. He did, however, have a long history of psychiatric problems for which he was service-connected from the military. He had been in treatment with almost every agency in town, but had refused to continue with any of them on a long-term basis. Medication had been both helpful and bothersome in the past. It was difficult to elicit a treatment request from the patient, and the staff felt that he was not in need of inpatient treatment. He agreed to try some low-dose neuroleptic medication but refused to follow through with an outpatient clinic appointment. During the next two years this patient would intermittently return to the emergency service, obtain a prescription for medication, and call to let us know how he was doing.

We do not intend to imply that this case represents the ideal treatment method for chronic schizophrenia, but it does offer an alternative system of care to clients who would otherwise receive little or no treatment. In working with this client, the goal of arranging for a more permanent outpatient treatment setting was always operative. Refusing to offer him medication unless he agreed to outpatient care seemed particularly harsh and likely to result in a power struggle. Thus, a combination of crisis care and transition care provided him with access to treatment while awaiting a change in his attitude toward outpatient care.

Emergency Treatment Modalities

The psychiatric clinician in an emergency service system relies on a select repertoire of intervention techniques.[6] Assessment of clients is fundamental in this type of work. Virtually all clients must receive a thorough evaluation of their problem and their request for care. Unlike the inpatient treatment setting, where the diagnostic list is exhaustive, the emergency service uses only a limited list of diagnostic labels.[7] This is useful in several ways. First, it keeps the clinician focused on the immediate issue which brought the client in for care and reduces the expectation that long-term problems can be resolved immediately. Second, in the context of a brief, one-time visit, the clinician views only a small segment of the client's behavior and therefore refrains from labeling clients with diagnoses that imply chronic mental illness, such as schizophrenia or borderline personality disorder. Nonetheless, the clinician must determine if the problem is the result of an organic condition, requiring medical evaluation, or if the client will be placed at risk if care is provided in an outpatient setting, when an inpatient setting would be a more protective environment.

Eliciting the client's request for care is valuable in securing desirable treatment resources and/or educating clients about necessary treatment programs. The work of Lazare and his co-workers is of unquestionable value to the emergency service clinician. Their conceptual model of the client as a customer structures the visit in a way that invites the client to discuss the need for care and the type of help that would be beneficial.[8] Although we may not always be able to comply with clients' requests, we can negotiate with them in an attempt to agree on a treatment plan of equal value.

Evaluating the client's problem and request for care remains a complicated task. While the emergency service may not focus on resolution of unconscious conflict and transferences, it is important to remember that these mechanisms are operative in our clients.[9] As the following case illustrates, the clinical diagnosis and the immediate problem may be two separate issues.

Clinical Example 1–2

The client was a 29-year-old single white female who had frequently presented to the emergency room for psychiatric care. She usually complained of nervousness and agitation. It was not difficult to elicit her long psychiatric history, which included multiple hospitalizations and outpatient treatment. She was currently in treatment at a local mental health center for both group and medication maintenance therapy. After the clinician had talked to her for some time, she finally revealed that her immediate problem was her group therapy. She had been transferred to another group because of her growing relationship with another patient in her former group. She requested that we contact her therapist and ask that she be allowed to return to her former group meeting.

In this situation, the client's immediate problem was not her chronic mental disorder but rather her inability to solve an immediate problem that had arisen in her therapy sessions. Providing her with some role playing and suggestions for approaching her therapist were well within the scope of emergency practice. Additionally, with the client's permission, her therapist was contacted the following day to facilitate her discussion of the problem with clinic staff. In the course of long-term psychotherapy or lengthy outpatient treatment, one can predict that impasses will occur. The emergency service is a safe alternative for clients to utilize during these times. Staff must remain sensitive to the transference issues, however, and attempt to reunite clients with their therapists whenever possible.

Another major modality within the psychiatric emergency service is to secure treatment resources for clients. Matching the client's problem, social and financial resources for treatment, and preference for treatment setting can be a delicate maneuver. It can also become the most rewarding aspect of the service in that it demands the greatest amount of creativity and flexibility by the clinician. In many instances the client's need for inpatient psychiatric treatment is obvious, but selection of a proper treatment setting may be difficult because of financial constraints, lack of available space, or the client's unwillingness to seek admission voluntarily. Outpatient resources for other clients may be difficult to secure because of waiting lists, catchment area restrictions, or transportation problems faced by the client.

In addition to maintaining open communication between the psychiatric emergency service and community programs, many emergency departments have extended their scope of practice for those clients who need outreach visits or who might resolve their problem in one or two return visits. Both transition care and crisis care are viable emergency service options when community resources are unable to provide these services.

The psychiatric emergency service clinician relies on assessment and evaluation skills, negotiates with clients for acceptable treatment options, is knowledgeable about community resources and their availability to clients, and utilizes brief treatment techniques. In the delivery of emergency care, an atmosphere of acceptance and willingness to resolve immediate problems is crucial. Clients are often open and receptive to talking about their problems, but still require some facilitation in developing the client–therapist relationship. In the context of one visit, the three phases of relationship development are present but abbreviated. In the *initial* phase, the client tells his or her story and the clinician evaluates the severity and etiology of the problem. This is also the critical time for developing a relationship, establishing a trusting environment, and educating the patient to psychiatric emergency services. The *working* phase conceivably applies to the therapeutic interventions and negotiations for treatment. Here the clinician applies intervention techniques likely to resolve the current problem or facilitates discussion of the need for further care and identifies the issues requiring treatment. Lastly, *closure* occurs, with the client and clinician discussing the alternatives for treatment and how to secure help with future problems.

Managing the milieu of the emergency service further defines the boundaries of the practice.[10] Clinicians forced to keep pace with the influx of clients frequently utilize triage principles to guide their decision making. Staffing limitations can be compensated for by screening clients quickly, seeing the most disturbed ones as soon as possible, and maintaining brief contact with those clients who are waiting to keep them informed of time delays and approximately when they will be seen. Utilizing other staff or accompanying family members can usually maintain an atmosphere of calm even when clients have little tolerance for frustration.

Since the focus of emergency psychiatric care is limited to immediate, here-and-now problems, treatment goals must be similarly restrained. This can be a difficult transition for psychiatric staff who are used to treatment settings which focus on making major changes in clients' behavior or have anticipated access to clients over several months of outpatient therapy. The role in emergency services is more analogous to that of facilitator, middle manager, or systems expert. The client's chief complaint and presenting behavior are understood from a diagnostic perspective, along with restrictions that might hinder further treatment. This evaluation ends with the formulation of a treatment plan that can be designed according to client and community resources.

Overview of the Text

The framework that we have used for this text is based on the therapeutic modalities previously outlined. The first step is the assessment process. Chapter 2 presents a modified assessment framework that develops hypotheses about the etiology and severity of the client's presenting problem. Guidelines are provided to assist the clinician with validation (or invalidation) of data before determining the most important problem faced by the client at the current time. As clinical example 2 pointed out, the client's psychiatric diagnosis (of chronic schizophrenia) may not be the presenting problem, but rather a contributing limitation to the resolution of a situational conflict (in this case an impasse in the therapy).

Determining treatment resources depends on several factors, such as client acceptance of the plan and the ability to follow through with referral options. A thorough assessment of risks such as suicidal or homicidal ideation must be made in conjunction with assets such as a supportive environment, available treatment resources, and previous success with treatment. Planning a course of action is dependent on the nature of the assets and liabilities inherent in each clinical situation. The client's clinical diagnosis adds a further dimension to this decision-making process.

Figure 1–1 depicts the decision-making process in psychiatric emergency care. The clinical problem is weighed according to the severity of the symptomatology. First, problems such as organic mental disorders and psychotic conditions usually have more severe symptomatology than situational conflicts or long-standing personality disorders. Second, risks such as suicide, homicide, or an inability to care for oneself are evaluated. These often determine the safety needs of the client or community and dictate the most appropriate treatment settings to protect each. Next, the assets, or enabling factors, which exist for the client will shift the direction that treatment options can take. Those clients with supportive environments or previous success with treatment will be more likely to benefit from care in a less restrictive environment, while severely disturbed, even dangerous clients without support systems may require more restrictive settings at the outset of treatment.

The goal of the decision-making model is to assist the clinician in formulating treatment plans in psychiatric emergency situations. The development of a treatment plan depends on the interaction of clinical data, since rarely does one portion of the clinical picture dominate the decision-making process. The delivery of emergency psychiatric care continues to be a complicated process secondary to the severity of clients' problems and the dirth of clinical resources to meet these clients' needs.[11]

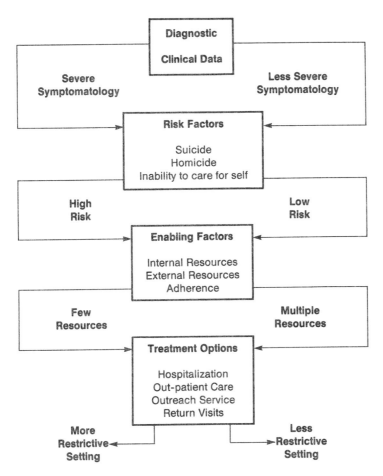

Figure 1-1 Decision-making steps in psychiatric emergency services.

One method for ordering the care in these services is the use of a framework that more evenly divides the clinician's attention among the most salient issues in emergency care. The issues have expanded from the initial focus on assessment and referral, to include increased treatment interventions by the emergency service and linkage with community-based programs. This has increased the scope of practice for the psychiatric emergency service.

Similarly, the movement away from formalized diagnostic labels allows the assessment process to focus on here-and-now remedial problems faced by the client. Thus, emergency psychiatric care has the potential to solve a wider spectrum of clients' psychological problems. As these programs mature over the years, it is reasonable to expect that psychiatric treatment principles would begin to be integrated into the care of clients in this setting.

Because clients are either in crisis or experiencing a psychological emergency, the treatment plan must include techniques appropriate for fragile individuals who are only marginally connected to a treatment setting. The use of holding beds and return visits to the emergency service are good examples of traditional therapies (e.g., inpatient and outpatient care) which have been modified for clients unable to obtain other services.

The remaining chapters of this book will discuss more fully the clinical content and application of the concepts of risk factors (e.g., suicide and dangerousness), enabling factors (e.g., internal resources, external resources, and interactional factors: adherence), and the assessment process unique to psychiatric emergency care settings. The integration of this material into viable treatment plans will be discussed at length in Chapter 9. The final chapter is devoted to a review of psychiatric emergency care models and their future usefulness in the delivery of mental health services.

References

1. Gerson, S., and Bassuk, E. L.: Psychiatric emergencies: An overview. *American Journal of Psychiatry, 137,* 1–11, 1980.
2. Zonana, H.; Henisz, J. E.; and Levine, M.: Psychiatric emergency services a decade later. *Psychiatry in Medicine, 4,* 273–290, 1980.
3. Craig, T. J.; Huffine, C. L.; and Brooks, M.: Completion of referral to psychiatric services by inner city residents. *Archives of General Psychiatry, 21,* 353–357, 1974.
4. Bassuk, E. L., and Gerson, S.: Into the breach. Emergency psychiatry in the general hospital. *General Hospital Psychiatry,* 1, 31–45, 1979.

5. Spitz, L.: The evolution of a psychiatric emergency crisis intervention service in a medical emergency room setting. *Comprehensive Psychiatry, 17,* 99–113, 1976.

6. Jacobs, D.: The treatment capabilities of psychiatric emergency services. *General Hospital Psychiatry, 5,* 171–177, 1983.

7. Spitz, L.: The evolution of a psychiatric emergency crisis intervention service in a medical emergency room setting. *Comprehensive Psychiatry, 17,* 99–113, 1976.

8. Lazare, A.; Eisenthal, S.; and Wasserman, L.: The customer approach to patienthood. *Archives of General Psychiatry, 32,* 553–558, 1975.

9. Kass, F.; Karasu, T.; and Walsh, T.: Emergency room patients in concurrent therapy: A neglected clinical phenomenon. *American Journal of Psychiatry, 136,* 91–92, 1979.

10. Talley, S., and Chiverton, P.: The psychiatric clinical specialist's impact on psychiatric emergency services. *General Hospital Psychiatry, 5,* 241–245, 1983.

11. Bassuk, E. L., and Schoonover, S. C.: The private general hospital's psychiatric emergency service in a decade of transition. *Hospital and Community Psychiatry, 32,* 181–185, 1981.

CHAPTER 2

ASSESSMENT OF THE CLINICAL PROBLEM

The first priority in psychiatric emergency care is assessment of the client's problem and the reason for seeking care. This may occur during the triage process in which the clinician must quickly determine the extent of the client's problem and the capacity to wait, or during the actual clinical interview in which a diagnostic assessment and care plan emerge. The clinician's responsibility is similar to that of other health care providers who must provide an atmosphere conducive to client disclosure and facilitate a descriptive account of the problem which lends itself to clinical diagnosis and intervention.

The assessment process actually encompasses three parallel agendas which ensure completeness and accuracy of the clinical data. First, the therapeutic alliance conveys the clinician's interest in helping the client and sets the stage for the client to trust the clinician with the information. Second, as the client tells his or her story, the clinician guides the interview in an attempt to clarify necessary facts for the psychiatric history and mental status examination. Third, the story and the clinical data form the basis for hypotheses about the problem which the clinician tests through additional questioning in the interview.

These clinical hypotheses should be broad enough to encompass the majority of clinical problems seen in psychiatric practice, yet narrow enough to keep the focus of care on here-and-now problems. The most concise list of hypotheses was developed by Lazare.[1] According to his model, clients' problems were explained by biological, behavioral, psychological, or sociocultural hypotheses and subsequently structured the intervention selected. Thus, if the clinical problem was depression, a biological hypothesis might indicate medication for treatment; conversely, a psychological hypothesis might suggest the use of psychotherapy to resolve underlying conflicts. As the clinician learns to develop hypotheses, the interview becomes a problem-solving session that seeks to understand the etiology and significance of the current symptoms.

In addition to utilizing a system of hypotheses to evaluate clients' problems, it is useful to rely on a diagnostic framework that is abbreviated. Although the psychiatric emergency service is represented by almost all diagnostic categories, interventions can be planned according to a select group of diagnostic labels, to avoid the search for a definite diagnosis which may later prove inaccurate given the limited client–clinician contact. The categories selected for our assessment framework are organic, psychotic, characterological, and situational problems. Their usefulness lies in their demarcation of the etiology, severity, and longevity of the client's problem/symptoms. The clinician again utilizes a problem-solving approach in determining the clinical significance of the data and guides the interview in directions which validate or refute each of the diagnostic labels. This will be discussed at length later in the chapter.

The search for psychopathology must be accompanied by an assessment of situational conflicts or precipitating events. These specific problems may become the focus of the intervention strategies and alert the clinician to long-standing themes which emerge under stress. The increased emphasis on treatment in psychiatric emergency services mandates that we address these crises and attempt to help clients find alternative coping mechanisms.

The skillful clinician is someone who has developed a system for organizing, identifying, and evaluating clinical data. The process of guiding the client's story while simultaneously searching for signs and symptoms of the clinical problem is fundamental to the assessment process. The subjective data presented by the client are coupled with more objective data obtained through the mental status examination and therapeutic interventions which test the client's capacity for therapeutic work. The chronological events that occur during the emergency visit provide an excerpt from the client's life which can be used as a reality check of the data obtained. These events can provide the clinician with valuable information on how the client arrived asking for help and tolerated the constraints of contact with a variety of health professionals. These differing vantage points allow the clinician to judge the internal consistency of the clinical data. In the final analysis, the identified clinical problem should account for the variance observed in the client's behavior throughout the visit and the interview.

Clinical Content

The Interview

The interviewing style and the goals of psychiatric emergency care require a modification of many traditional approaches used in psychological treatment. Unlike traditional psychodynamic psychotherapy, which relies on a process of eliciting the client's story and attending to unconscious manifestations, the evaluation process is aimed more directly at the immediate problem. The alliance with the therapist, which is useful in developing the transference for long-term psychotherapy, is restrained in the emergency room setting to facilitate the client's attachment to psychological care providers in general. In this way, the client is helped to understand the nature of the clinical problem which precipitated contact with the emergency service, and is socialized in regard to the process of therapeutic work with another therapist, if necessary.

These modifications in therapeutic style are not without theoretical constructs. Margulies and Havens noted that the therapeutic alliance of the existential and interpersonal theorists facilitates the data collection process through empathy and counterprojective techniques, respectively.[2] Both techniques capitalize on the therapist's ability to experience the world as the client presents it, and to utilize the defenses inherent in the client's repertoire to access valuable clinical material. The value of the therapeutic relationship must be tempered by the restrictions of any relationship that prevents each member from disclosing data that are considered unacceptable to the other. The emergency visit, however, allows psychiatric emergency clinicians to capitalize on the client's sense of urgency and emotional pain which precipitated the contact. While the client's defenses may be more permeable at this time, caution must be exerted to prevent the client from excessive disclosure, which often causes withdrawal (sealing over), making subsequent therapeutic work more difficult.

Another style, or modification in style, is the eclectic approach. Although this approach was once considered a "jack of all trades, master of none" style, there is now renewed interest in it.[3] To this end, there is greater responsibility on therapists to utilize a variety of therapeutic modalities which complement the client's ability to do therapeutic work. Contributions from the behavioral and cognitive therapies have reduced therapy time by directly focusing on cognitive/behavioral deficits acquired by clients and assigning tasks for overcoming maladaptive patterns. These intervention techniques guide the evaluation inquiry by focusing on issues amenable to therapy.

The psychiatric emergency service model restricts (or broadens) the therapist's approach toward an eclectic one. With a multitude of clinical problems likely to emerge during the assessment process, the clinician must be able to move quickly toward a medical model approach if the client is psychotic or organically impaired; and conversely, to direct the anxious, depressed client to the areas of psychological conflict and repressed material responsible for the emotional pain. With little uniformity in the client population likely to seek care in the emergency service, a variety of requests for care will emerge. Thus, the onus is on the clinician to establish an atmosphere where the client's psychological code can be deciphered and agreed upon by both parties.

The structure of the interview must match the pace and content of the client's story. Generally, the interview has phases, with the client talking more in the beginning, the therapist discussing and reviewing more toward the end, and balanced participation at closure when planning is finalized. Exceptions to this pattern depend on the particular psychological distress of the client. Allowing long, painful silences with depressed clients is antitherapeutic, as is a rambling, incoherent monologue from a psychotic client. The subtle structure provided by the therapist facilitates the disclosure of important material and controls the tempo of the interview, while interventions are aimed at reducing or increasing emotional distress to enhance the problem-solving process.

Diagnostic Categories

Virtually all psychiatric diagnostic categories are represented in the adult population seen in psychiatric emergency services.[4] The clinician must therefore possess an extensive knowledge of presenting symptoms in major psychiatric classifications in order to direct the interview. Although the accuracy of first-evaluation diagnoses might be questioned, there is little doubt that the emergency service is a gateway to inpatient and outpatient psychiatric treatment settings. The deinstitutionalization movement in mental health has increased the usage of psychiatric emergency services.[5] A reduction in state hospital beds and in the length of stay in these settings, in conjunction with a saturation of community mental health service systems, has resulted in increased numbers of chronically mentally ill clients living in communities without easily accessible mental health support systems. These individuals constitute a large portion of the chronic repeater group seen in the psychiatric emergency service.[6] For these clients, the assessment process shifts from an emphasis on the primary diagnosis to a determination of acute exacerbations, medication reactions, or precipitating events that have destabilized the client's fragile coping mechanisms. Indeed, it is often beneficial to notify the treating therapist to inquire about recent crises, changes in treatment protocols, and therapist vacations.

An emphasis on neuropsychiatry has prompted recent studies documenting the medical needs of psychiatric clients. Careful screening of clients in state hospitals and outpatient psychiatric clinics has found the incidence of medical illness to vary from 9 to 58% in the populations studied.[7-10] Upwards of 50% of these medical conditions were missed by the referring agency or the client's physician.[11] Additionally, researchers estimate that a substantial number of these medical conditions cause or exacerbate the psychiatric symptoms.[12] Another group of medical-surgical disorders were unrelated to the psychiatric symptoms but required medical treatment.

The list of medical conditions diagnosed in these psychiatric patient populations is quite exhaustive, and alerts the clinician to the need for medical evaluation of clients arriving for psychiatric care. Attention is focused on those conditions likely to simulate psychiatric symptoms, as well as disorders that might arise from psychiatric treatment (e.g., drug-related movement disorders and medication reactions), the client's poor living conditions, or age-related illnesses likely to go unattended secondary to their silent nature (e.g., hypertension, diabetes mellitus, and malignancies). Table 2–1 lists the physical systems most frequently associated with psychiatric symptoms.[13] The most effective screening procedures in diagnosing these conditions were a 34-panel blood chemistry test, complete physical examination, the psychiatric history, and a complete blood cell count.

One obvious difficulty for the clinician in the psychiatric emer-

TABLE 2-1   Frequency of Medical Illness by Physiologic System and Relationship to Psychiatric Symptoms

SYSTEM	CAUSED OR EXACERBATED SYMPTOMS	UNRELATED	TOTAL
Endocrine	28	3	31 (17%)
CNS	12	. . .	12 (6%)
Cardiovascular	6	7	13 (7%)
Hematologic	12	3	15 (8%)
Gastrointestinal	4	5	9 (5%)
Genitourinary	1	9	10 (5%)
Respiratory	. . .	6	6 (3%)
Musculoskeletal	1	14	15 (8%)
Multiple system	14	61	75 (40%)
Total	78 (42%)	108 (58%)	186

Source: Hall, R. C. W.; Gardner, E. R.; Stickney, S. K.; et al: Physical illness manifesting as psychiatric disease. II. Analysis of a state hospital inpatient population, *Archives of General Psychiartry* 37:989–995.

gency service is determining which clients are most likely to have an organic etiology for their psychiatric condition. One method of screening clients is the use of medical staff in the emergency service to "clear" clients prior to their psychiatric evaluation.[14] This arrangement, however, has two serious shortcomings. First, clients' disruptive behavior often precludes a thorough evaluation; second, the emergency service is not oriented toward routine screening examinations in the absence of a differential diagnosis. More appropriately, medical staff can be used as consultants once the suspicion of a medical disorder is confirmed by the psychiatric staff. In this way, the medical evaluation can proceed in a less random manner.

The Psychiatric History

The psychiatric history focuses on those areas of the client's life that are most likely to reflect emerging psychological problems. Table 2–2 lists the areas typically covered in a psychiatric history. The interview begins with the client's chief complaint or reason for seeking care. Some clinicians note this statement in the clinical record because it succinctly describes the client's complaint. It also alerts the clinician to the client's level of insight into the current problem. Obviously, as the interview progresses, more pertinent information emerges and clarifies the immediate issues.

The history of the present illness documents the actual events, symptoms, and concerns of the client that caused him or her to seek care at this particular time. The source of these data is usually the client, except in situations in which the clinical problem has diminished the client's capacity to provide coherent information. When this occurs, it is important to obtain this information from the family, therapist, or another community agency.

The components of the psychiatric history most useful in psychiatric emergency situations are a developmental history, an overview of the client's interpersonal relationships, family dynamics which influence the developmental environment, an intrapsychic or ego assessment, and current life events which precipitated the immediate problem and disrupted the client's baseline level of functioning. These items are listed in Table 2–2, with specific areas of inquiry for the clinician.

The psychiatric history guides the interview toward landmark events likely to illustrate the etiology of the client's problem. Obviously, each clinical problem will have different patterns of data for each of the categories listed above.

The psychiatric history also documents previous psychiatric treatment and the duration of the current problem or its premorbid course. This is a critical factor when determining an exacerbation of

TABLE 2–2   The Psychiatric History

  I. *Chief complaint*
 II. *History of the present illness*
      A. Onset/duration of symptoms
      B. Precipitating events
      C. Evolution of the problem
III. *Social and developmental history*
      A. Physical and emotional development
      B. Cognitive development
      C. Current developmental tasks
      D. Interpersonal relationships
      E. Constancy and relatedness
 IV. *Family dynamics*
      A. Nuclear family relationships
      B. Family environment/losses
  V. *Intrapsychic/ego assessment*
      A. Reality testing
      B. Self-esteem
      C. Social competence
 VI. *Current life situation*
      A. Occupational/financial
      B. Attainments/losses
      C. Constancy
VII. *Past psychological problems*
      A. Perceived help
      B. Source of help

---

an established psychiatric condition or long-standing characterological disorder. Similarly, the clinician determines whether or not the psychiatric symptoms represent a classical picture indicative of psychopathology or, conversely, have emerged during a stressful period.

The presenting pattern of psychiatric symptoms and the premorbid functional state of the client are useful markers in differentiating psychological from organically induced syndromes. Most psychiatric disorders, with the exception of depression, have defined periods of high-risk and premorbid behavioral patterns indicative of emotional distress. Therefore, symptoms that arise outside of these time frames in individuals who have good premorbid adjustment alert the clinician to search for organic precipitants.

The Mental Status Examination

The mental status examination (MSE) is a systematic evaluation of psychological and cognitive phenomena. Table 2–3 lists the specific items in a typical MSE and the data obtained. The examination can be divided into two portions; one tests psychological phenomena and the other formally tests cognitive functions.

Part I: Psychological

Observational skills are sufficient for the evaluation of appearance, affect, and speech. The client's thought processes are reflected in speech, but more direct questioning is required to determine the presence of delusional material, thought withdrawal, or thought insertion. Perceptual disturbances are also best evaluated by direct

TABLE 2–3   The Mental Status Examination

I. Psychological evaluation
   A. Appearance: dress, behavior, physical characteristics, affect
   B. Speech: quality, quantity, and organization
   C. Affect/mood: facial expression, subjective report
   D. Thought processes: clarity, organization, symptomatology
   E. Perceptual disturbance: hallucinations, illusions
II. Cognitive evaluation
   A. Orientation: person, place, and time
   B. Fund of knowledge: recent and past events
   C. Attention and concentration: calculations and serial tests
   D. Memory: immediate, recent, and remote
   E. Abstract reasoning: proverbs and similarities
   F. Judgment and insight: understanding the need for care

---

questioning. Here the clinician inquires about hallucinations, illusions, or depersonalization/derealization experiences. The observation of affect should be compared with the client's subjective report of mood.

Observational data are important clues to the underlying clinical problem or psychiatric disorder. By comparing the client with an idealized norm comprised of the client's occupational, demographic, educational, ethnic, and sociocultural characteristics, the clinician can determine what if any deviations exist and if these are attributable to a psychological dysfunction. The value of creating a mental image of the client's characteristics is that it allows the clinician to identify the source of the deviations. In some cases, these deviations may be related to counterculture affiliations or current fads, and thus are unrelated to psychopathological conditions.

Much care needs to be exercised in assigning value judgments to MSE data. Many discrepancies exist secondary to poverty, anxiety, and ethnic influences. Conversely, setting a standardized norm for comparison purposes prevents overidentification with traits similar to those of the clinician.

Part II: Cognitive

The cognitive portion of the MSE is useful for detecting learning disabilities and neurological disorders. Many psychiatric clinicians utilize the cognitive section to rule out organic differential diagnoses during the evaluation. Specific areas tested are orientation, fund of knowledge, memory, attention and concentration, abstract reasoning, judgment, and insight. (See Table 2-3 for the items tested under each of these categories.) It is critical that the clinician promote optimal testing circumstances. This is done by eliciting the client's cooperation and explaining the purpose of the questions being asked. This procedure avoids creating a hurried atmosphere wherein the client may feel foolish and suspicious of the clinician's motive for asking such obvious questions as "What is the date?" or "Who is the president?"

The Medical History

The previously cited studies documenting the prevalence of undetected medical conditions in psychiatric patient populations make screening with a brief medical history useful in identifying high-risk clients. Inquiry about health status, medication use (and abuse), previous medical/surgical conditions, and health care practices alerts the clinician to potential organic etiologies which may explain the immediate problem. The medical history is particularly valuable in screening clients without the classical signs and symptoms of mental illness and with a history of good emotional adjustment.

Specific items included in a medical history are listed in Table 2-4. Whenever possible, each of these areas should be investigated during the interview. It is common to find elderly clients taking multiple medications or medically ill clients not taking prescription drugs as ordered. Acute changes in psychological functioning can occur secondary to medical problems, drug interactions, electrolyte imbalances, or a previously undiagnosed medical condition. The detection and treatment of medical conditions coexisting with newly diagnosed psychiatric symptoms should delay the search for a psychiatric disorder until the medical condition is stabilized.

Physical Evaluation

The emergency room does not lend itself to complete or even screening physical examinations in the absence of suspicious biological etiologies. There are, however, techniques to evaluate the client's overall health status to detect underlying physical problems. By using systematic observational skills, the clinician can determine the status of many medical and neurological functions. Additional data can be gathered by monitoring vital signs and direct questioning.

The functions obtained by a noninvasive physical evaluation are listed in Table 2-5. These are gait, motor strength, coordination, facial and general body symmetry, skin color, weight distribution, nutritional status, hair and nail conditions, and an overall impression of how well or ill the client appears to be. The age and sex of the client also direct the clinician to search for those conditions which are specific to gender and certain periods in the life span.

The most important point here is that the clinician should remember that medical conditions are frequently associated with spe-

TABLE 2–4   The Medical History

General health status
Previous medical/surgical conditions
Injuries
Medication use
Health care practices
Occupational hazards

TABLE 2–5   The Physical Examination

Gait
Motor strength
Coordination
Facial and general body symmetry
Skin color
Weight distribution
Nutritional status
Hair and nail condition
Wellness versus illness

cific psychological symptoms, and that the evaluation process must
rule out biological etiologies.

Summary

The evaluation process need not be complicated. There are standard
areas of inquiry in psychiatric practice which facilitate and organize
the data collection process. In the model we have developed, it seems
most important to organize the problem-solving process around
steps that lead the clinician toward one of four diagnostic categories.
The specific areas of inquiry are then detailed according to the information most likely found for each diagnosis or clinical problem. In
this way, the clinician is guided toward a clinical hypothesis while
simultaneously ruling out the other diagnostic possiblities. This both
simplifies the steps and safeguards against a narrow evaluation.

Clinical Assessment Model

In this section, we will outline the model and the inquiry process
which accompanies it. It is important to note that the clinician has
the following responsibilities in the evaluation process: First is the
development of the therapeutic alliance. Second is guidance of the
clinical interview, which facilitates the client's disclosure of clinical
material. Third is the internal problem-solving process, which further directs the validation of clinical hypotheses through specific
data collection (see Figure 2–1).

The diagnostic framework that we have outlined is composed of
four clinical diagnoses: organic, psychotic, situational, and characterological problems. While these do not represent all of the DSM III

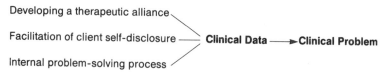

Figure 2–1 The evaluation process.

labels, they are sufficient for emergency evaluation and care planning. Data elicited during the interview are evaluated according to a severity index, allowing the clinician to validate initial impressions of the clinical problem.

While the assessment process aims to identify which if any of these clinical problems are present, it simultaneously allows the remaining hypotheses to be eliminated. In this way, the clinician refrains from early closure on the problem-solving process by moving toward alternative hypotheses before terminating the clinical investigation. This is important since many psychological symptoms could be explained on the basis of stressors in the client's life, thus narrowing the search for organic or long-standing characterological problems.

The model is listed in Figure 2–2. The first step focuses on observational data. Items of importance are attire, verbal presentation, emotional/affective state, eye contact, motor behavior, and physical appearance. By attending to these data early in the interview, or even before meeting with the client, the clinician begins to develop hypotheses about the nature of the problem. For example, the age of the client and his or her physical appearance can quickly direct the initial inquiry.

The client brought in by the police who is combative and wearing only a blanket, will require a very different approach than a quiet, casually dressed person who is waiting patiently in the examination room. The most important message to convey to beginning clinicians is that a wealth of clinical data can be gathered and utilized once one develops a system for organizing information.

Step One

Each of the areas listed in the first portion of the model will be discussed according to the information most relevant to obtain during the assessment process. Specific questions are listed under each category to guide the clinician's problem-solving process.

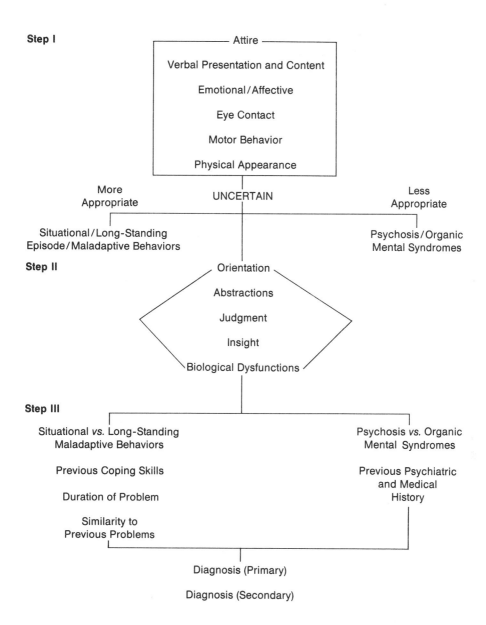

Figure 2–2   Clinical assessment model.

Attire

This item includes the information from the MSE category of appearance. Here the clinician evaluates what the client is wearing for clues about how well the client is able to care for himself or herself.

Is the client completely and appropriately dressed for both the occasion and the weather?

Does the style of dress match the stereotype of the client?

Does the choice of clothing represent a functional purpose or a counterculture group?

Does the type of clothing convey a message about or from the client?

Evaluation of attire directs the clinician toward those psychiatric conditions likely to affect the client's ability to care for the self or otherwise distort the client's self-image. Variations unrelated to psychopathological conditions can arise from poverty, counterculture affiliations, and personal choice. The most useful clinical data detect dementing or delirious conditions, schizophrenia, depression, and drug use. These latter conditions affect attire through declining ability/interest in personal hygiene, weight loss/gain, and eccentric choice of clothing.

Verbal Presentation

Speech is an important representation of thought processes. The functions of speech listed in the MSE category are evaluated here. Again, this is an important item in the differential diagnosis of organic conditions.

Does the language and structure of the verbal content match the socioeconomic background, education, and ethnicity of the client?

Is the content clear and well organized?

Does the content match the behavior of the client?

Is the content easily conveyed to the clinician, and does it follow the general structure of the interview?

Variations in speech may reflect organic conditions such as stroke or intoxication. Additionally, evidence of a thought disorder, delusional material, or psychotic thinking will be apparent in the content of the client's story. Normal variations may indicate different cultural and educational backgrounds, as well as slang phrases peculiar to fads or specific age groups. Poverty of speech may indicate depression or severe loss of self-esteem. Less obvious disturbances of thought may be noted in clients' eccentric or idiosyncratic use of language.

Emotional/Affective State

Here the clinician notes the facial expression of the client and then proceeds to assess the underlying mood. Normally, there should be agreement between the client's affect and underlying mood. Similarly, the evaluation of facial expression can alert the clinician to facial asymmetry, alcoholic conditions, or other organic physical disorders which affect skin condition and weight distribution (e.g., myxedema, Cushing's syndrome, cirrhosis).

> Does the affective state match the clinical problem discussed by the client?
> Is the range of affect appropriate for the situation?
> Is there a change in affect during the interview that is inconsistent with the material presented?
> How does the client's affect/mood make the clinician feel?

Affective states alone are rarely diagnostic of psychopathological conditions. Anxiety may prevent the client from easily disclosing personal data early in the interview, but this usually abates once an atmosphere of trust and acceptance is established. Manic or depressive states are more easily reflected by the client's emotional state. Conversely, an absence of affect may be attributed to schizophrenia or dementing processes that have dulled the client's ability to display emotion toward others. Here the clinician's own response to the client is a useful barometer in determining how engaging the client can be with another person.

Eye Contact

The client's ability to establish and maintain eye contact with the examiner reflects not only underlying self-esteem but also the influence of competing phenomena. For example, clients with visual and auditory hallucinations may be attending to other stimuli, and thus may appear preoccupied during the evaluation. Seizure disorders may be recognizable by the client's repetitive eye movements, and drug actions may be best observed by their effect on pupil size or nystagmus.

> Can the client maintain a normal amount of eye contact?
> Does he or she appear to be attending to other stimuli in the environment?
> Is there any evidence of biological influence over the client's ability to maintain eye contact?

Eye contact is one measure of the client's ability to interact with the examiner during the interview. Only rarely will it determine the actual underlying psychiatric problem. Nonetheless, it is a useful marker of both interpersonal skill and biological dysfunction.

Motor Behavior

The mannerisms and overall level of behavior will help the clinician identify problems which are manifested psychomotorically. Psychiatric conditions affect behavior by either increasing or decreasing the client's usual amount of activity. Medical conditions also bring about variations in the usual patterns and behaviors of clients.

Is the client's behavior goal directed?
Is there evidence of increased or decreased activity?
Does the client's behavior seem irrational or eccentric?

Observation of the client's behavior includes patterns, mannerisms, and gestures which may identify the etiology of the disorder. Normal variations may occur during times of anxiety or secondary to long-standing habits. Diminished activity may result from medical problems such as stroke or fatigue, or from psychiatric conditions such as depression. Hyperactivity may result from mania, drug reactions, or psychotic processes.

Physical Appearance

Physical appearance, like attire, gives the clinician access to valuable information about the client's overall health status. It also marks the client's ability to provide self-care in the recent past. There are several specific areas to be noted under physical appearance: hygiene, weight, nutritional state, general level of well-being, skin color, hair growth, obvious signs of recent or past injuries, and vital signs (respiration, pulse, and increased temperature).

Is the client clean and well cared for?
What signs are there of past injuries or illnesses?
Does the client appear ill or malnourished?
Does it seem likely that the client's physical appearance is related to a psychiatric disorder or responsible for the current conditon?

This evaluation phase can be valuable in revealing underlying organic conditions. Clients who have become ill quickly are more likely to have biological etiologies or catastrophic events in their lives. Many chronic psychiatric conditions are responsible for marked changes in health and hygiene which are noted here.

Evaluation of Step One

At this point in the evaluation, the clinician has begun to organize the clinical material into levels of severity. Clients appear either very disturbed or more able to participate in the interview and share their problems with the clinician. Those clients who are unable to discuss their problems, instead displaying signs of underlying pathology, would be judged more incapacitated. These are the clients likely to have clinical problems caused by organic or psychotic etiologies. Those clients who are engaged in the interview process and able to define their current difficulties are more likely to have characterological or situational problems. A more difficult group to evaluate are those clients brought in by concerned others, who resist or cover their problems during the evaluation process.

This process of differentiating the problem according to level of severity ultimately guides the interview process. Without a marker for the direction of the interview, the clinician wanders aimlessly through the spectrum of clinical questions, rather than identifying patterns of behavior and clinical data that rule out other clinical problems. This is not the stage of the interview where hypotheses are validated or refuted, but rather where directions are set for the remainder of the time. One should remember that the data collected should not only justify the identified clinical problem, but refute the alternative clinical hypotheses.

Step Two

The second step in the assessment process utilizes selected techniques from the MSE, the medical history, and the physical examination to refine the clinician's diagnostic hypotheses. At this stage, the clinician may well have determined that the features of the client's story and the behavioral attributes indicate more or less severe psychological symptomatology. These next levels of inquiry further define the most likely clinical diagnosis.

It is important, however, to remember that the clinical diagnosis and the reason for seeking care may be separate. While the client may have an existing psychiatric diagnosis such as schizophrenia or borderline personality disorder, the precipitating event may be a situational crisis which warrants primary attention.

The items in step two were chosen because of their ability to distinguish between psychotic and organic mental disorders, as well as situational problems. As a general rule, the client with less severe psychopathology (e.g., situational or characterological problems) should perform well on these items. Conversely, the psychotic or organically impaired client will not do well in some of these areas.

Orientation

Testing the client's orientation to person, place, and time is vitally important in screening those clients with dementia or other physical conditions that affect mentation. In order to elicit the most accurate data from the client, the instructions/directions for these questions should be clear and should emphasize the reasoning behind the inquiry to avoid resistance from the client.

Does the client know the name of the setting that he or she is in?
Does the client seem to understand the function of the setting?
Is the client oriented to time (e.g., date, month, year, season, time of day)?
Can the client tell you his or her name and significant demographic data?

The client with a dementing illness or delirium will often display the greatest impairment in one or more of these categories. Declining abilities usually affect time first, then place, and lastly person. The psychotic client may do poorly on these questions as well, but the answers are usually bizarre rather than incorrect. The client who claims to be Jesus Christ is not disoriented to person, but evidences a delusional belief about his identity.

With experience in evaluation methods, clinicians often weave these questions into the general conversation rather than formally assessing the client's orientation. However, the organically impaired client may retain a wide range of social skills that mask an underlying cognitive impairment. Therefore, any suspicion of organic impairment should direct the clinician to test this area formally.

Abstraction

The ability to abstract is usually tested through proverbs and similarities on the MSE. Here the client is given a proverb and asked what the message or meaning of the saying is. In testing similarities, two objects with similar traits are presented, and the client is asked to tell the examiner what is the same about them. Both psychotic and organic conditions diminish the client's capacity for abstract thinking, making the problem-solving process more concrete. Clients without this type of impairment should have little difficulty understanding the directions for these tests and giving appropriate answers.

> Can the client understand the testing directions?
> Is there evidence of an ability to conceptualize similar traits between objects?
> Are proverbs abstracted to common levels of meaning?
> Does the task elicit rambling, incoherent descriptions from the client?

Evaluation of the client's performance on these tests must include some assessment of those factors likely to interfere with completion of the assigned task. Anxiety, educational variables, and cultural differences may prevent clients from understanding the proverbs, thus decreasing their ability to call on previous experience to decipher the inherent message.

Previous experience with these types of questions may improve the results for chronically ill psychiatric clients, but this effect will usually be clear to the clinician after the history of psychiatric treatment has been gathered.

Insight and Judgment

These two items are considered together because of the subjective nature of the evaluation process. The clinician must determine if the client is thinking appropriately and would approach everyday problems with a logical, problem-solving style. Therefore, the value of assessing these functional capacities in clients lies in the picture that one develops about how well the client can understand his or her current problems and the coping mechanisms employed to solve daily impasses.

> How well does the client understand his or her psychological problems?
> What explanations does the client give for having emotional difficulties? .
> Does the client rely on socially acceptable problem-solving techniques for resolving difficult situations?
> Can the client engage in a psychologically focused discussion about the clinical problem?

Clients with psychotic or organic conditions may experience difficulty in gaining insight about their problems. This occurs secondarily with the process of being out of touch with reality; in the case of organic impairment, the client no longer recognizes the cognitive deficits. While the client with a characterological problem is not out of touch with reality in the same way that a psychotic client is, there is usually a reduction in problem-solving capacity because the protective defense mechanisms are primitive or underdeveloped. In this case, the clinician notes patterns of poor adaptation or projection/ blaming of external factors for the emotional difficulties encountered.

Biological Dysfunctions

The previous categories in step two primarily evaluate the cognitive processes in clients. This is useful in documenting the presence of cognitive deficits not readily apparent in the interview process. This last category is a final attempt to establish a potential biological etiology to explain the psychological symptoms. The use of medical history questions is applicable here and will alert the clinician to high-risk clients.

> What age- or gender-related health problems are most likely to occur in this client?
>
> Are there signs of poor physical health?
>
> Does the past medical history or life-style of the client cause a predisposition to immediate health problems?
>
> Is there any potential for misuse or abuse of existing medical regimens?
>
> What medical conditions could account for the psychological problems experienced by the client?

A thoughtful analysis of the above questions allows the clinician to think through any biological hypotheses regarding the client's clinical problem. The emphasis on biological etiologies is not intended to dilute the psychological inquiry, but rather to balance the problem-solving process and avoid single explanations for emotional distress. Medical and psychiatric problems may coexist and require prioritization in planning treatment approaches.

Evaluation of Step Two

The use of selected MSE questions and a final search for biological precipitants will usually be sufficient for second-level hypothesis testing. At this level, the clinician should be fairly definite in determining the severity of the client's psychological problem. Thus, any remaining diagnostic dilemmas would arise from confusion over whether the client had a situational crisis or characterological problem, or, in the case of more severe psychopathological disturbance, had an organic versus a psychotic problem.

In step three, the clinician's task centers on more refined diagnostic impressions leading to the primary and secondary clinical diagnoses. The stepwise model is not intended to guide the clinical interview, which should be structured by the clinical material being shared by the client and the tempo of the interview itself. Instead, these steps are designed to organize the mental operations of the clinician that separate clinical data into compartments representative of the four diagnostic categories.

Step Three

The final step in the assessment process differentiates situational from characterological problems and organic from psychotic processes. The decision-making steps are different for each set of clinical problems. For less severe problems, the clinician seeks to understand the client's previous coping mechanisms, the duration of the current problem, and any similarity between the current difficulty and previous problems experienced. The differentiation between organic and psychotic problems utilizes the past medical and psychiatric histories to help the clinician determine the likelihood of an exacerbation.

Situational versus Characterological Problems

When the interview process is exclusively focused on the client's difficulty with situational problems, interpersonal conflict, or family problems, the clinician must determine if this is a crisis or a psychiatric emergency. The term *crisis* is used to describe situations which have overwhelmed the functional coping abilities of individuals. A *psychiatric emergency* refers to recurring distress in individuals with preexisting characterological difficulties. There are three points of distinction between situational and characterological problems: 1) frequency of the event, 2) level of defense utilized, and 3) primary versus secondary nature of the problem. With situational problems, the client is usually entering the system for the first time, having utilized the defenses in his or her repertoire to cope with a new problem. In contrast, the client with a characterological problem has used the system previously for care, and returns when primitive defense mechanisms fail. Thus, the problem is secondary to long-standing deficits in coping abilities.

Previous Coping Mechanisms

One of the major distinctions between situational problems and characterological difficulties is the ability to maintain adequate defense mechanisms for solving problems. The client with a personality disorder often lacks mature coping skills. Thus, when faced with new or threatening situations, anxiety mounts and regressive behavior appears. When there is severe psychopathology, as in the case of borderline or antisocial disorders, the client's level of distress reaches psychiatric emergency proportions. Suicidal behavior, threats to others, or destructive acts may be some of the first-line attempts to reduce emotional distress and obtain emotional attachment to others. The following questions may assist the clinician in evaluating the client's abilities and liabilities in coping with distress.

How has the client coped with previous stressful situations?
Is there a past history of emotional difficulties?
How extensive is the client's repertoire of coping behaviors?
Are the client's defense mechanisms primitive or mature?
Has the client had to cope with similar situations, or is the current one novel and unfamiliar?
Does the severity of the stressor match the distress experienced by the client?

Comparison of the client's response to the situational problem and knowledge of the client's psychological abilities gives the clinician some idea about the reason for the emotional distress. Where the client's response seems out of proportion to the situational event, there is a high degree of suspicion that a characterological disorder or previously unresolved problem might exist. If the client had an established pattern of successful emotional adjustment, the situational problem might be of catastrophic proportions.

Duration of the Problem

When the situational problem has existed for some time, the clinician should inquire about the reasons for seeking care at this particular time. This line of questioning not only clarifies the actual precipitant but also highlights recurring themes in the client's life that magnify the current problem. The client with a situational problem typically does not seek immediate care when faced with a psychologically stressful event. The history often reveals a series of problems that have occurred within a short period of time and the attempts by the client to solve them, either alone or with the help of supportive others. Only when the usual efforts have failed do these individuals appear for help. The client with a characterological problem, on the other hand, is more likely to seek help sooner, particularly if he or she has become attached to the mental health care delivery system. Here the pattern of repeated emotional difficulties emerges, alerting the clinician to personality deficits.

What attempts has the client made to solve the immediate problem?
Has the client been able to tolerate the emotional distress for a reasonable period of time?
Were the coping mechanisms employed successful in reducing emotional distress?
Does the client want help in learning how to cope with the problem, or merely relief from the emotional distress experienced?

This part of the evaluation process helps the clinician determine if the client has some tolerance for frustration and delay of gratification with respect to emotional discomfort. The normally functional individual delays in seeking help until the usual coping behaviors are no longer useful. Conversely, the client with a personality disorder becomes more distraught under less threatening circumstances and lacks a sense of personal security in being able to handle the problem.

Similarity to Previous Problems

The client with a situational problem will have difficulty coping because the situation is new and calls for skills not previously learned/needed. The client with a characterological problem will have repeated difficulties with similar situations which have become associated with unresolved conflicts.

Are the events reported by the client similar to previous difficulties?
Is there a history of successful resolution of these types of problems?
Is there a theme to the emotional conflicts in the client's life?
How much growth has the client attained in coping with the problem?
What has prevented successful resolution of the problem?

The primary objective of the clinical inquiry is to establish the extent to which the client has adapted to the stressors inherent in daily living and adopted adequate coping skills. Characterological disorders usually prevent clients from resolving conflicts in an organized, systematic way to protect themselves from a feeling of devastation created by impasses and impending or real failures.

Psychotic versus Organic Problems

The differentiation between these two diagnostic categories is primarily aimed at helping the clinician determine the etiology of the presenting symptoms. It is usually clear that the client's level of distress is high, but doubt might remain about the causative factors. The most useful data come from past psychiatric and medical histories. These allow the clinician to make predictions about existing conditions which have the potential to recur.

Past Psychiatric History

The major psychiatric conditions, such as schizophrenia, manic-depressive illness, and borderline characterological disorders, are known to have chronic courses. Thus, it is likely that clients known to have one of these diagnoses will experience recurrent emotional problems. Although this fact does not preclude the coexistence of a medical problem, it makes it easier to predict the etiology of the immediate problem.

> Does the client have an established psychiatric diagnosis?
> Is the client receiving psychiatric treatment and complying with the prescribed regimen?
> Do the current symptoms mimic those of the existing disorder?
> Is the previous psychiatric problem the primary reason for the immediate visit, or does it play a secondary role?

Identification of previous psychiatric problems alerts the clinician to vulnerabilities in the client's social/emotional functioning. Therefore, even with an established psychiatric label, the evaluation process must consist of more than merely relabeling an existing problem. This is particularly important in clients with manic-depressive illness or schizophrenia, who may not tolerate situational conflicts even with maximal psychiatric intervention. For these clients, the emergency visit may constitute an appeal for added emotional support.

Past Medical History

Previous medical problems, surgical procedures, or injuries may be of great importance in determining the etiology of the psychological problem. A host of conditions are likely to cause emotional and cognitive changes that are indistinguishable from psychological problems. Thus, the clinician should take the time to inquire about the client's medical history in order to rule out the possibility of an organic differential diagnosis.

> Are there medical problems or a family history of problems known to cause psychiatric symptoms?
>
> Is the client taking medications known to affect cognition or emotions?
>
> Is there evidence of injuries prior to symptom formation or likely to emerge later?
>
> Does the client have a chronic illness that is poorly controlled?
>
> Has the client been treated for an illness known to recur?

Documentation of medical problems may not always determine the etiology of the current problem, but it arouses suspicion of underlying physiological pathology that might require attention. Depending on the severity of the medical problem, it might take precedence over psychiatric care in the treatment plan.

Evaluation of Step Three

The third step in the assessment model is designed to aid in the final differentiation between conditions with less severe and more severe psychopathology. The major distinction between situational problems and characterological disorders involves the client's previous ability to solve emotional conflicts. Those clients who have been unable to tolerate emotional distress are more likely to have underlying personality disorders.

The more disturbed client is likely to have a psychotic illness or decompensation secondary to an organic illness which has affected cognitive and emotional abilities. Determining past medical and psychiatric conditions allows the clinician to narrow the final hypothesis.

Summary

The decision-making steps outlined in the assessment model are designed to help the clinician organize the data into hypotheses which are validated or invalidated at each step in the process. The first step grossly evaluates the severity of the client's behavior and the verbal account of the immediate problem. As the clinician clarifies the clinical history and problem, the hypotheses shift toward one side or the other of the model.

The second step offers additional clarification about how functional the client is. The MSE and a search for biological etiologies distinguish clients with major impairments from those with personality or behavioral limitations which prevent maximum coping ability.

The third step deepens the assessment process and distinguishes situational from characterological problems or psychotic from organic problems. As the clinician begins to make closure on this portion of the assessment process, it is important to note that any combination of the four diagnostic categories might become the primary or secondary problem identified. The primary problem should become the priority for resolution, while the secondary one is a contributing problem. For example, the client who is psychotic due to an organic problem might require medical care prior to controlling the psychotic behavior. Conversely, a client with a less severe organic dysfunction might proceed with psychiatric care and schedule a medical evaluation for a later time.

Case Example

The following evaluation case is presented to describe both the flow of content in a clinicial interview and the decision-making process that the clinician uses to validate or refute hypotheses.

Prior to meeting with the client, the clinician notes that the client has voluntarily signed into the emergency service and requested psychiatric care. He is waiting patiently in the interview room after briefly talking with the triage nurse.

> PNS: Good morning, my name is _____, and I am the psychiatric nurse in the emergency service. Can you tell me what brings you in today?
>
> CL: I need help. Last night I lost my temper and beat up my wife, and destroyed the inside of my living room.
>
> PNS: Has this happened before?
>
> CL: Yes, but not as bad as this time.
>
> PNS: Tell me what was worse about this time.
>
> CL: I'm not sure, but I felt more out of control than in the past.
>
> PNS: What happened to set things off last night?
>
> CL: Nothing unusual. We were discussing finances, arguing some, and then I lost control.
>
> PNS: What do you remember about what happened?
>
> CL: I hit my wife a few times, broke some lamps in the living room . . . things like that.
>
> PNS: How badly is your wife hurt?

CL: She's bruised, but otherwise o.k.

PNS: Tell me about the other times this has happened.

CL: When I was in the service I got into some fights, and at work I've lost control with some of the guys and began fights.

PNS: Have these fights usually occurred when you have been drinking?

CL: Yes, most of the time . . . but I'm not usually very drunk.

At this point, the differential clinical hypotheses might include characterological problem, including alcohol abuse with loss of control, impulse disorder, or an organic differential of rage attacks. The possibility of recurrent situational losses is also a potential problem. A psychotic differential diagnosis is less likely because of the client's fairly clear account of the problem and lack of any evidence of a thought disorder or peculiar description of the problem.

PNS: Tell me about your current life situation.

CL: This is my third marriage. I'm not working right now.

PNS: When were you married before, and what caused these relationships to end?

CL: I was married for a couple of years when I was twenty, then I got married again at age twenty-seven, and this last time a couple of years ago.

PNS: What caused these marriages to fail?

CL: Well, we just didn't get along well . . . too much fighting.

PNS: What kind of work do you do?

CL: I usually work in some type of plant . . . loading things, that kind of work.

PNS: How is it that you are not employed now?

CL: Well, I got into a fight with my boss and stormed off the job.

PNS: How much alcohol do you use?

CL: I don't drink every night, but when I drink, it's usually only beer. Maybe four or five at a time.

Using the clinical assessment model as a framework, the following data were obtained by the psychiatric nurse specialist in the interview thus far. The client was casually dressed, clean, and cooperative in the interview. His verbal presentation was logical and well organized, although somewhat limited in detail. His eye contact was initially poor (he was looking around the room), but in time he began to tolerate more eye contact with the nurse. His affect was constricted, sad, or tense, and he seemed genuinely concerned about his current problem. He had no unusual mannerisms, and the amount of motor behavior was appropriate for the situation. His physical appearance was not indicative of acute illness, but he did have a scar along the left temporal area of his skull. At this stage of the data collection process, the interviewer might conclude that this 30-year-old male was in a moderate amount of emotional distress secondary to an episode of loss of control. He seemed interested in obtaining psychiatric care, as evidenced by his voluntarily seeking care and his relative cooperation in the clinical interview. It is also likely that he has a characterological disorder, as evidenced by his numerous marriages, inability to control his temper, and poor work record.

Using the second step in the assessment model, the following data emerged. He was oriented to person, place, and time and able to abstract proverbs and similarities, but lacked some insight into the cause of his problem. The physical findings were more pronounced.

> PNS: The scar on your head . . . can you tell me what happened?
> CL: I got into a fight about six months ago and had a blood clot. It had to be removed surgically.
> PNS: Are you taking any medication or had any problems since the surgery?
> CL: No, only an occasional headache.
> PNS: Do you ever notice that you smell foul things that are not present?
> CL: How do you know that?
> PNS: Tell me what you have experienced.
> CL: Over the last few weeks, I've noticed that I smell things, but I can't figure out where they are coming from.
> PNS: Have you had any other experiences that you can't explain?
> CL: No, I don't think so.

This extra amount of data leads the clinician to consider an organic hypothesis for the client's difficulty. While this is not a complete answer to the problem, since the client had these outbursts before the injury a few months ago, it does raise the possibility of a problem requiring medical attention. Obviously, the client also has poor impulse control and alcohol abuse as potential problems, but these might better be listed as secondary or contributory to the outbursts of rage at this time.

References

1. Lazare, A.: Hypothesis testing in the clinical interview. In: Lazare, A. (ed.), *Outpatient Psychiatry*. Baltimore: Williams & Wilkins, 1979, pp. 131–140.

2. Margulies, A., and Havens, L. L.: The initial encounter: What to do first? *American Journal of Psychiatry*, 138, 421–28, 1981.

3. Karasu T. B.: Recent developments in individual psychotherapy. *Hospital and Community Psychiatry*, 35, 29–39, 1984.

4. Gerson, S., and Bassuk, E.: Psychiatric emergencies: An overview. *American Journal of Psychiatry*, 137, 1–11, 1980.

5. Bassuk, E.: The impact of deinstitutionalization on the general hospital psychiatric emergency ward. *Hospital and Community Psychiatry*, 31, 623–627, 1980.

6. Raphling, D. L., and Lion, J.: Patients with repeated admissions to a psychiatric emergency service. *Community Mental Health Journal*, 6, 313–318, 1970.

7. Hall, R. C. W.; Popkin, M. K.; DeVaul, R. A.; et al: Physical illness presenting as psychiatric illness. *Archives of General Psychiatry*, 35, 1315–1320, 1978.

8. Karasu, T. B.; Waltzman, S. A.; Lindenmayer, J.; Buckley, P. J.: The medical care of patients with psychiatric illness. *Hospital and Community Psychiatry*, 31, 463–471, 1980.

9. Davies, W. D.: Physical illness in psychiatric outpatients. *British Journal of Psychiatry*, 111, 27–33, 1965.

10. Koranyi, E. K.: Morbidity and rate of undiagnosed physical illness in a psychiatric clinic population. *Archives of General Psychiatry*, 36, 414–419, 1979.

11. Koranyi, E. K.: Physical health and illness in a psychiatric outpatient department population. *Canadian Psychiatric Association Journal*, 17, 109–116, 1972.

13. Hall, R. C. W.; Gardner, E. R.; Stickney, S. K.; LeCann, A. F.; and Popkin, M. K.: Physical illness manifesting as psychiatric disease. II. Analysis of a state hospital inpatient population. *Archives of General Psychiatry*, 37, 989–995, 1980.

14. Weissberg, M. P.: Emergency room medical clearance: An educational problem. *American Journal of Psychiatry*, 136, 787–790, 1979.

CHAPTER 3

DECISION MAKING IN CLINICAL ASSESSMENT

In the previous chapter, the assessment framework was discussed in terms of specific data obtained during the clinical interview which were organized into a framework leading to the clinical problem. Clinical decision making, on the other hand, addresses the *process* of assigning clinical significance to the data collected. In this step, single items of data are woven into a collective data base. This collective data base is more than the sum of individual parts since a picture emerges based on the clinician's clinical judgment.

Using Janis and Mann's model of decision making, the clinician makes an appraisal of the data based on knowledge of psychopathology and human behavior, and determines the significance of this information in terms of its likelihood to put the client at risk or facilitate resolution.[1] A secondary appraisal determines the need for available treatment resources. The decision-making style of their model most applicable to psychiatric emergency care is one of "vigilance." Janis and Mann define this as the highest level of interest in information seeking, characterized by "active search for supportive and nonsupportive information, with careful evaluation for relevance and trustworthiness; preference for trustworthy nonsupportive information if threats are vague."[2]

In order for the clinician to arrive at a clinical judgment about the client's presenting problem, three factors must be present. First is a *knowledge base of psychological problems* and their behavioral/cognitive representations. This information guides the interview by the constellation of signs and symptoms known to coexist in different clinical problems. Second is a *method for collecting data.* In psychiatric practice, the clinician relies on interviewing skills, the mental status examination, and the psychiatric history. Third is an *internal classification system* which validates the reliability of the clinical judgment. Based on clinical experience, consultation, education, and supervision, the clinician comes to trust the significance of his or her own impressions of clinical material.

This chapter will focus on the knowledge base for each of the four clinical problems (psychotic, situational, characterological, and organic) used in the Assessment Model. First, a general profile of clients with each of these problems will be presented in order to demonstrate the constellation of clinical data common to each problem area. Second, a comparison of the four clinical problems will be presented using the areas of the assessment framework from Chapter 2. Each comparison will detail the differences (or similarities) among the data from the four clinical problems. Since clients' psychiatric diagnoses may be only a contributing factor in the psychiatric emergency visit, chronic but stable psychological problems will be woven into the discussion of each clinical problem. In this way, the clinician is reminded that more than one problem may exist at a time, and treatment strategies might focus more directly on only one issue at a time.

Clinical Profiles

Decision making in psychiatric practice usually relies on symptom constellations and the severity of symptoms in planning treatment strategies.[3-5] These symptoms are usually present during the clinical interview and dictate much of the client's behavior in attending to the interviewer's inquiries. Similarly, the history of the current problem identifies those conditions with definable courses of onset. For chronic conditions with remissions and exacerbations, the history can be helpful in predicting the recurrence of a chronic condition. Another area of inquiry is the strengths and weaknesses in the client's psychological and social lives, which determine the baseline level of functioning and previous attainments of high-level wellness.

This latter dimension clues in the clinician about the expected degree of possible adjustment and avoids attempts to minimize the client's potential for improvement or plan interventions beyond the scope of psychiatric emergency care. Lastly, the presence of other psychiatric disorders forces the clinician to decide if the immediate problem is an exacerbation of underlying pathology or secondary to diminished coping abilities. If the chronic condition is maximally stabilized, a secondary level of care should be directed at helping the client cope with the problem as if it were a situational crisis. If, on the other hand, the underlying psychiatric condition is not well controlled, tertiary-care strategies are directed at treating the primary condition, be it a psychotic, characterological, or organic problem.

Each of the clinical profiles will be discussed according to the aforementioned criteria. General information will be presented about the client's interview behavior, symptom constellation and severity, history of the current problem, psychological and social strengths and weaknesses, and other diagnoses that might contribute to the problem.

Situational Problem

Situational problems may occur at any time during the life span. There is, therefore, no age of onset or likely period of time when these issues may arise. Similarly, there are few restrictions on the kinds of problems clients may find overwhelming. Examples include, but are not limited to, marital discord or divorce, death in the family, employment problems or unemployment, termination of a relationship, financial concerns, academic problems, grief reactions, family dysfunction, and interpersonal relationship problems.

Clients appear seeking help with these problems during times of extreme stress or after a self-determined period of waiting has failed to reduce the psychic pain they are experiencing. The interview process quickly focuses on the precipitating event secondary to the client's ability to share psychological material in the hope of obtaining guidance from the clinician.

When the problem is primarily a situational crisis, the flow of information to the clinician is moderately clear, although the sequence of events may be distorted by anxiety and the client's inability to see clear connections between the event and the disproportionate degree of emotional discomfort. As the interview (and the story) unfolds, greater comfort is perceived in the client if the clinician has been successful in understanding the client's distress. Opportunities for problem solving are apparent, and the clinician is usually able to move from assessment inquiries to actual therapeutic suggestions or interpretations.

The client's symptoms are rarely of psychotic proportion. Instead, feelings of anxiety, depression, fatigue, tearfulness, and insomnia may dominate the clinical picture. Functional roles such as spouse, parent, employee, and companion may suffer from the client's inability to concentrate fully emotional energy on others. Self-destructive behaviors such as smoking, alcohol use, overeating (or undereating), and withdrawal from others who are a source of support may increase. Suicide may be attempted during extreme distress, but usually as a last resort.

The history of the client's psychological adjustment is good. Realization of life goals can be found in the premorbid history, although these achievements will vary with socioeconomic, intellectual, and financial endowments. The client will also have passed the usual developmental milestones with a minimum of difficulty. When these developmental milestones occur simultaneously with a situational crisis, the emotional response may be exaggerated secondary to the synergistic effect of the two events.[6] Therefore, adult developmental frameworks such as Levinson's[7] and Sheehy's[8] are helpful in predicting ongoing developmental work, which might explain the client's inability to cope at a particular time.

Previous life experiences may also contribute to the current situational problem in the form of unresolved themes which recur in the client's life. Identification of these themes by the clinician can facilitate greater understanding of the dynamics of the immediate problem and the client's understanding of the importance of previous psychological events. Similarly, anniversary reactions, particularly grief responses, may actually be the precipitating event that surfaces during the inquiry process. It is not uncommon for these unresolved themes and anniversary reactions to go unnoticed by the client who has repressed the emotional pain connected with past events.

Evaluating the client's strengths is best accomplished by an ego assessment. Bellak and Small's framework for ego assessment focuses on 12 areas of ego function. These are listed in Table 3–1, along with the components of each item.[9]

In addition to these areas of ego function, the clinician notes the defense style and personality traits of the client. Typically, the client has a fairly flexible style of coping and utilizes a range of defensive maneuvers in managing various emotional states.

Lastly, in psychiatric emergency care, the clinician should not

TABLE 3–1   Ego Functions and Their Components

Ego Function	Components
1. *Reality testing*	Distinction between inner and outer stimuli Accuracy of perception Reflective awareness and inner reality testing
2. *Judgment*	Anticipation of consequences Manifestation of this anticipation in behavior Emotional appropriateness of this anticipation
3. *Sense of reality and sense of self*	Extent of derealization Extent of depersonalization Self-identity and self-esteem Clarity of boundaries between self and world
4. *Regulation and control of drives, affects, and impulses*	Directness of impulse expression Effectiveness of delay mechanisms
5. *Object relations*	Degree and kind of relatedness Primitivity (narcissistic, anaclitic, or symbiotic-object choices) Degree to which others are perceived independently of oneself Object constancy
6. *Thought process*	Memory, concentration, and attention Ability to conceptualize Primary-secondary process
7. *Adaptive regression in the service of the ego*	Regressive relaxation of cognitive acuity New configurations
8. *Defensive functioning*	Weakness or obtrusiveness of defenses Success and failure of defenses
9. *Stimulus barrier*	Threshold for stimuli Effectiveness of management of excessive stimulus input
10. *Autonomous functioning*	Degree of freedom from impairment of primary autonomy apparatuses Degree of freedom from impairment of secondary autonomy
11. *Synthetic-integrative functioning*	Degree of reconciliation of incongruities Degree of active relating together of events

TABLE 3–1   continued

Ego Function	Components
12. *Mastery-competence*	Competence (how well the subject actually performs in relation to his existing capacity to interact with and actively master and affect his environment)
	The subjective role (subject's feeling of competence with respect to actively mastering and affecting his environment)
	The degree of discrepancy between the other two components (i.e., between actual competence and sense of competence)

Source: Reproduced with permission of Bellak, L. and Small, L.: *Emergency Psychotherapy and Brief Psychotherapy.* New York: Grune & Stratton, 1978, pp. 56-57.

underestimate the value of searching for situational problems in clients who have existing psychiatric diagnoses. The most innocuous event may overwhelm a client with a psychotic disorder and lead the inexperienced clinician to search for preexisting psychiatric symptoms rather than helping the client identify potentially solvable problems. Discovery of these events requires a directed search for social changes in the client's life. The client may have to be asked about specific situational conflicts and events in order to elicit the information.

Affective and characterological disorders also weaken ego functions, rendering the client more vulnerable during stressful periods. Thus, the search for stressful precipitants should parallel the inquiry for psychopathological signs and symptoms.

In cases in which the client has a previously identified psychiatric disorder, the critical task of the clinician is to determine the magnitude of the emotional distress and the degree to which the client is maximally involved in other psychiatric care. If the client has utilized emergency services in addition to ongoing therapy, the focus may shift to provision of immediate psychotherapeutic interventions until access to the established therapist can be arranged.

Characterological Problem

Characterological problems constitute a large proportion of the psychiatric clinician's caseload.[10] Clients with these problems frequently experience recurring intrapsychic and interpersonal conflicts that propel them toward care providers. Personality traits which become defined as disorders develop early in adult life (i.e., between 16 and 18 years of age) and become manifest during critical periods of real or feared threat. Unlike those with personality types or traits considered normal, the client with a personality disorder has a fixed, inflexible style which restricts emotional growth through behavior patterns aimed at reducing emotional turmoil rather than expanding psychological potential. The client fails at interpersonal relationships, adult developmental mastery, and moral development in normal environmental circumstances secondary to the constraints imposed by an inflexible personality style.[11]

Table 3–2 lists the current types of personality disorders from the DSM III and the most prominent feature distinguishing one disorder from another.[12] While assessing the dominant personality style, the clinician must also note the degree of impairment or success in each of the following areas:

Interpersonal relationships
Tolerance for closeness and warmth toward others
Independence/dependence in relationships
Empathic understanding of others' needs
Tolerance for the rules and conduct of societal norms
Frustration tolerance/delay of gratification.[13,14]

These inter/intrapersonal dynamics are common denominators in all personality styles and vary little over time.

Unlike the client with a situational difficulty who approaches the psychiatric emergency service requesting help with a particular problem, the client with a personality disorder is focused on his or her level of distress and demands amelioration of symptoms. The presentation of clinical material begins with symptoms of distress or implied threats of self-destruction in the face of conflict and anxiety. Unable to ask directly for help, the client often attempts to force the clinician to provide care or protection from harm. This action is in contrast to that of clients who are able to engage in a problem-solving process wherein the evolution of the current difficulty is revealed.

What becomes clear to the clinician during the interview is the client's *style* of sharing information and relating to the clinician. Signs of impulsivity, ambivalence in closeness versus guardedness, suspiciousness of others' motives, and an underdeveloped sense of self-concept are readily apparent in the client with a characterological disorder. The configuration of personality deficits and assets de-

TABLE 3–2   Types and Features of Personality Disorders (DSM III)

PERSONALITY DISORDER	DISTINGUISHING FEATURE
Paranoid	Suspiciousness and mistrust of others
Schizoid	Inability to form social relationships and indifference to others
Schizotypal	Odd, eccentric thinking, behavior, speech, and perception
Histrionic	Overly dramatic, intensely expressed behavior
Narcissistic	Grandiose sense of self-importance and exhibitionistic need for constant attention
Antisocial	Violation of others' rights and failure to obey social norms
Borderline	Marked instability in interpersonal behavior, mood, and self-image
Avoidant	Hypersensitivity to rejection, humiliation, or shame
Dependent	Passive relinquishment of responsibility and lack of self-confidence
Compulsive	Perfectionism, indecisiveness, and restricted expression of emotion
Passive-aggressive	Indirect expression of resistance to demands for adequate work and social performance
Atypical, mixed, other	Alternate modes of personality disorder presentation using a new description or combining existing disorders

Source: Reproduced with permission of the American Psychiatric Association, Diagnostic and Statistical Manual of Mental Disorders, Third Edition, Washington, D.C., APA, 1980.

termines the precise personality disorder. This is of less importance, however, in emergency care than the actual determination that the problem is a characterological one in general.

Symptoms are frequently severe secondary to the level of distress experienced by clients when their usual defensive structure is insufficient to contain their anxiety. Psychotic symptoms may emerge in the form of diminished reality testing, severe affective disturbance, suicidal or homicidal ideation, and labile behavioral manifestations secondary to poor boundaries and rigid defense mechanisms. Much of the symptomatology displayed is intended to reduce emotional distress and engage the interest and support of others considered important by the client. This demand for support and attention is often labeled as "manipulative" by the clinician and results in a nontherapeutic countermaneuver of withdrawal/withholding of empathy. These countertransferential feelings can be useful for *assessment* purposes, but interventions should emanate from an understanding of the psychodynamics of the disorder and thus aim to contain some of the anxiety.

Labeling the problem as characterological is dependent on the identification of long-standing traits established during adolescent or early adult developmental periods. Variations among clients will depend on the degree to which the personality style has been effectively integrated into the life plan. Those clients with more intact ego functions will have integrated their dominant personality traits into adaptive social and occupational roles. Psychological distress appears when life structures change, as in termination of a relationship or employment role changes, and the client is forced to rely on alternate problem-solving styles. Less-well-functioning individuals will be unable to utilize their personality traits in the service of social and occupational roles; instead, they will spend most of their emotional energy in protecting their fragile intrapsychic structure.

Collapse of the client's functional ability indicates that an excessive threat has been noted by the client and that secondary attempts at anxiety reduction have been ineffective. The client's adaptive style is unable to respond with alternative defensive maneuvers to handle the new level of threat. Like the psychotic client, the client with a characterological problem is likely to respond with acting-out behavior, withdrawal, and social instability. This is not unexpected if one remembers that the client is unable to respond to stress in any fashion other than the predominant defensive style of the character trait.

Decision making is perhaps most difficult when there is a suspicion of an underlying characterological problem. Psychotic symptoms in borderline clients are common, and yet they will dominate the clinical picture. Additionally, when clients have both psychotic and characterological diagnoses, intervention strategies might be limited by the uncooperative style of the client. Lastly, the presence of organic problems such as dementia or epilepsy may distort the client's personality traits to such an extent that interventions are dependent on the characterological structure when the organic dysfunction is irreversible.

Psychotic Problem

Psychotic symptoms are rarely diagnostic of a particular psychiatric dysfunction. They may occur secondary to organic illness, characterological traits, or specific psychiatric problems. Therefore, once it has been determined that psychotic symptoms are present, the clinician must again generate hypotheses about their etiology. In this section, the emphasis will be on those psychiatric conditions known to cause psychotic symptoms such as schizophrenia and affective disorders. A general discussion of the effect of psychotic symptoms on the client's psychological capabilities will also be included.

Schizophrenia

The usual age of onset for schizophrenic illness is late adolescence or early adulthood. The progression of this disorder is usually chronic, with remissions and exacerbations of symptoms. According to the DSM III diagnostic criteria for schizophrenia, there must be a six-month period of declining psychological abilities before the client can be labeled schizophrenic.[15] This prevents misdiagnosis of clients whose psychotic symptoms are secondary to reactive psychotic episodes or affective disorders.

In clinical practice, clients with schizophrenia usually have several psychotic episodes, with remissions of varying success. Many clients will continue to experience psychotic symptoms even after stabilization with psychiatric treatment. Thus, clinicians working in outpatient settings become skilled in caring for clients with chronic psychotic symptoms, but in psychiatric emergency care the clinician must determine the potential for controlling these symptoms and the client's capacity to function in the community.

Psychotic symptomatology is not difficult to detect once the client has become severely disturbed and less guarded in sharing delusional/hallucinatory experiences. As the psychotic experience increases for the client, the ability to separate reality experiences from psychotic ones decreases. With those clients who are in the early stages of experiencing psychotic ideas or have learned to guard against sharing these ideas for fear of being labeled mentally ill, the examiner must be particularly skillful in eliciting the data. Additionally, clients with isolated psychotic symptoms may also be reserved in sharing these experiences with others.

The client's behavior during the interview will range from obviously psychotic to a more controlled, guarded presentation of the problem. The chronically ill client may experience a recurrence of hallucinations and delusional ideas that is frightening. First-admission psychotically disturbed individuals may be brought in by family members' or the police once their behavior has become uncontrollable. As a general rule, the client's story is difficult to follow if there is evidence of a thought disorder. This disorder prevents the client from organizing thoughts; instead, circumstantial and tangential thinking is displayed.

Like the range of presentations in characterological conditions, psychotic symptoms may also include paranoid, aggressive, grandiose, or autistic variations. If the client's problem is particularly difficult to understand, the interview might better focus on MSE questions. This provides the clinician with a structured approach in investigating the presence (or absence) of hallucinations, delusions, affective changes, or other unusual experiences. If the interview is structured, there is less pressure on the client to organize an unstructured interpersonal contact with an unfamiliar person.

Assessment of clients with psychotic symptoms requires great skill and empathy by the clinician. The client must feel safe, both from intrusion and from abandonment. Similarly, the clinician needs to structure the *process* of the interview in order to maintain the client's boundaries and contact with reality. Without contradicting the unreal psychotic material directly, the clinician must strive to orient the client to the reality of the here-and-now situation. In this way, clients are afforded maximal opportunity to comply with the assessment process and avoid aggressive behavior in order to protect themselves.

The current DSM III criteria for a diagnosis of schizophrenia include one of the following:

> Bizarre delusions,
> Somatic grandiose, religious, nihilistic or other delusions without persecutory content,
> Delusions with persecutory or jealous content,
> Auditory hallucinations in which either a voice keeps up a running dialogue . . . or two or more voices converse with each other,
> Auditory hallucinations on several occasions with content of more than one or two words, having no apparent relation to depression or elation, or
> Incoherence, marked loosening of associations, markedly illogical thinking, or marked poverty of content of speech if associated with at least one of the following:
>> Blunted affect, delusions/hallucinations, or catatonic or other grossly disorganized behavior.[16]

In addition to these specific criteria, the client must evidence a prodromal phase of deterioration or a residual period of withdrawal, poor social performance, blunted affect, bizarre ideation, or continued perceptual disturbances.

Affective Disorders—Mania

Clients typically experience their first manic episode before the age of 30.[17] Like schizophrenic disorders, manic episodes are likely to recur throughout the life span once the illness is established. There is, however, greater stability in the client's emotional/social functioning during remissions. Manic episodes are usually associated with depressive syndromes, either immediately or at another time in the client's life. Depressive episodes, however, may occur without accompanying manic behavior.

Manic episodes are chronic conditions, although the use of lithium has greatly reduced the number of repeated episodes in clients who respond favorably to the drug. Changes in both physical health and psychosocial events may precipitate manic behavior, since clients are particularly vulnerable to increased stress/pressure. Thus, the presence of increased stress should not be construed as a situational problem since manic symptoms tend to escalate once they recur.

Manic symptoms are also fairly easy to assess, since the client's behavior is markedly disturbed by the elevated mood. Clients in a manic state are pressured in speech, thought, behavior, and drive. Although some of these symptoms may be mood incongruent, the client is usually satisfied with these feelings of power, energy, and increased self-esteem. Those clients with an established diagnosis may recognize a recurrent episode, whereas clients experiencing their first episode usually must be urged by others to seek psychiatric care. Thus, it is not uncommon for these clients to arrive at the psychiatric emergency service involuntarily.

The client's story is less useful than the constellation of symptoms. Psychotic symptoms such as delusions and hallucinations *may* occur in manic episodes, but as a rule the presenting picture is more likely to exhibit disturbances of mood, behavior, and self-esteem. The client's capacity to control these symptoms is low, requiring increased structure from the clinician during the interview. The actual number and severity of the symptoms will vary among clients; however, the clinician will be able to evaluate even the most uncooperative client since most of the behavior is objectively evaluated. Since extreme agitation may be caused by organic conditions, it is important that other causes (e.g., amphetamine use) for the behavior be investigated.

The current DSM III criteria for a diagnosis of manic behavior include the following:

> One or more distinct periods with a predominately elevated, expansive, or irritable mood.

Duration of at least one week . . . during which, for most of the time, at least three of the following symptoms have persisted:

Increase in activity,
More talkative than usual,
Flight of ideas,
Inflated self-esteem,
Decreased need for sleep,
Distractibility, or
Excessive involvement in activities that have a high potential for painful consequences which is not recognized, e.g., buying sprees, sexual indiscretions, foolish business investments, reckless driving.[18]

There should not be any residual or preexisting symptomatology suggestive of schizophrenia or organic illness that could account for the symptoms.

Affective Disorders—Depression

Unlike schizophrenia and manic disorders, which have age-specific periods of onset, major depression can occur at any time during the life span. Recurrent episodes of depression are likely to occur, and their frequency of repetition is directly correlated with the amount of residual impairment in social/occupation role functions.

Depression is a common human emotion. Thus, assessment of the client with depressive features must be complete, and must document the severity of the symptoms and/or the need for a protective treatment environment. Suicidal behavior and malnutrition secondary to weight loss are the two most serious consequences of major depressive episodes.

In addition to the depressive mood, there may be evidence of psychomotor retardation or agitation. The client may easily express depressive feelings, although there can be a paucity of thought and speech in severely depressed clients. A common experience for clinicians is their own notably depressed mood after evaluating a depressed client.

One of the more distinguishing features of major depressive episodes is the client's loss of self-worth and the feeling of being a bad, almost evil person who deserves to die. This is in marked contrast to normal fluctuations in mood experienced by individuals in their daily lives. The onset of severe depressive symptoms may be secondary to situational events, but the magnitude of the response is clearly beyond normal human experiences. The client may be unable to give an account of his or her current problem. Instead, the depressive symptoms dominate the clinical picture, and the client's behavioral repertoire is similarly restricted.

The current DSM III criteria for diagnosis of major depressive disorder include the following:

> Dysphoric mood or loss of interest or pleasure in all or almost all usual activities and pastimes.
>
> At least four of the following symptoms have each been present nearly every day for a period of at least two weeks . . . :
>
> Poor appetite or significant weight loss or increased appetite or significant weight gain,
> Insomnia or hypersomnia,
> Psychomotor agitation or retardation,
> Loss of interest or pleasure in usual activities or decrease in sexual drive not limited to a period when delusional or hallucinating,
> Loss of energy; fatigue,
> Feelings of worthlessness, self-reproach, or excessive or inappropriate guilt,
> Complaints or evidence of diminished ability to think or concentrate, such as slowed thinking, or indecisiveness not associated with marked loosening of associations or incoherence,
> Recurrent thoughts of death, suicidal ideation, wishes to be dead, or suicide attempt.[19]

Like the criteria for diagnosis of manic disorders, these symptoms should not be explainable on the basis of an organic illness or coexist with symptoms of schizophrenia during periods of remission.

The actual variation in psychotic symptoms can be accounted for by the specific diagnostic classifications just presented. Affective disorders are considered psychotic when the client is unable to perform normal role functions secondary to mood, behavior, and self-esteem changes. For these clients, the reality of their internal world is distorted by the predominant mood change (e.g., depression or mania). By comparison, clients with schizophrenia have distorted the meaning of external events and perceptual experiences to accommodate their psychotic thinking.

In the acute phase of these disorders, psychological strengths are masked by the psychotic symptoms. The history of the immediate problem notes the premorbid level of adjustment and determines the most useful treatment setting. As noted earlier, chronic psychotic symptoms may not prevent clients from immediately returning to the community, although their severity is often directly correlated with the decision to hospitalize.

There is a significant overlap between psychotic symptoms and other psychological problems. Situational crises may precipitate underlying manic, depressive, or schizophrenic symptoms. The severity of these psychotic symptoms precludes problem-solving efforts until the client is stabilized. Organic illness also has the potential to produce psychotic symptoms that mimic those of functional psychiatric states. If the medical condition can be treated, these symptoms usually abate. If the medical condition has a chronic, deteriorating course (e.g., Wilson's disease, Huntington's chorea, or Parkinson's disease), the client may eventually require primary management by psychiatry to control the refractory psychiatric symptoms.

Organic Problem

Organic conditions can precipitate psychological symptoms at any time during the life span. These symptoms are not limited to psychotic phenomena, since anxiety, mild depression, and character pathology are known to herald the onset of numerous medical conditions.[20] This poses a problem for clinicians, since there is little if any difference between the psychiatric symptoms of organic conditions and those produced by psychological disorders. Therefore, an organic differential diagnosis should be considered for *all* clients seen in the psychiatric emergency service.

One method for determining the likelihood of an organic condition is identification of the known risk factors for each client. The following criteria will refine the assessment process in detecting organic problems:

Current health status—signs of illness, dental care, and nutrition

Known age- and gender-specific illnesses likely to occur

Recent medical/surgical/traumatic illnesses

Drug use: prescribed, over the counter, illegal, alcohol use

Premorbid level of social/psychological adjustment

Thus, for *each* client, there is an index of potential risk from undetected medical problems.

Suspicion is aroused when the psychological symptoms appear out of context with known patterns/constellations of psychiatric disorders. This reaction is useful only for those psychiatric conditions with well-established classical presentations and ages of onset. Another method for detecting organic etiologies is by attending to inconsistencies in the client's history. For example, clients with a history of good psychological adaptation who suddenly become emotionally unstable without evidence of a catastrophic crisis would require medical evaluation. It is highly unlikely for individuals to suddenly develop severe psychiatric problems after many years of functional adjustment. If the emotional changes are acute, the clinician considers those medical problems known to occur suddenly. If their onset is more gradual, the clinician would consider those conditions with insidious subclinical phases.

Tables 3–3 and 3–4 list the medical conditions known to produce psychotic and depressive symptoms, respectively.[21,22] The most common types of medical problems that produce psychological symptoms are endocrine, neurological, metabolic/hematologic, infectious, and nutritional problems. Untoward drug reactions, drug interactions, and toxic levels of prescribed medications are also known to induce psychiatric symptoms. Since many of these conditions have lengthy subclinical phases, clients may experience less se-

TABLE 3–3   Organic Causes of Psychosis

Endocrine
    Hyperthyroidism
    Hypothyroidism
    Cushing's disease
    Addison's disease
    Hyperparathyroidism
    Uncontrolled diabetes mellitus

Neurological
    Wilson's disease
    Huntington's chorea
    Parkinson's disease
    Cerebrovascular accident
    Seizure disorder:
        partial or complex
    Hypertension
    Brain tumor; metastases
    Alzheimer's/Pick's disease

Metabolic/hematologic
    Anemia
    Porphyria
    Hyponatremia
    Uremia
    Systemic lupus erythematosis

Infectious
    Encephalitis
    Tertiary syphilis
    Meningitis
    Brain abscess
    Herpes simplex encephalitis

Nutritional
    Pellagra
    Wernicke-Korsokoff's syndrome
    Vitamin B_{12} deficiency

Drugs/medications
    L-Dopa
    Steroids
    Disulfiram
    Reserpine
    Amphetamines
    Digitalis
    Anticholinergics
    Hallucinogenics
    Bromides
    Alcohol
    Tricyclic antidepressants

Traumatic
    Subdural hematoma
    Postconcussion
    Postcraniotomy

TABLE 3–4   Organic Causes of Depression

Endocrine
  Hypothyroidism
  Hyperthyroidism (elderly)
  Addison's disease
  Cushing's disease
  Hyperparathyroidism
  Postpartum states

Neurological
  Alzheimer's/Pick's disease
  Parkinson's disease
  Huntington's chorea
  Multiple sclerosis
  Wilson's disease

Metabolic/hematologic
  Hypokalemia
  Hyponatremia
  Hypercalcemia
  Anemia
  Congestive heart failure

Infectious
  Subacute bacterial endocarditis
  Mononucleosis
  Postencephalitis
  Pneumonia
  Influenza
  Tuberculosis
  Hepatitis

Nutritional
  Pellagra
  Folic acid deficiency

Drugs/medications
  Alcohol
  Barbiturates
  Lead poisoning
  Methyldopa
  Birth Control Pills
  Reserpine
  Propranolol
  Steroids
  Digitalis

Other
  Pancreatic/bowel cancer
  Oat cell cancer

vere emotional symptoms (e.g., anxiety, mild depression, and fatigue) in the earlier stages of the illness.

Intellectual/cognitive impairment is clearly associated with organic etiologies. Signs of delirium or dementia are easily documented by the use of the MSE. Table 3–5 lists the common causes of dementia and delirium, and differentiates between conditions producing reversible and nonreversible dementia.[23,24] Although the workup for reversible causes of dementia is not within the realm of psychiatric emergency care, referral of clients to a suitable treatment setting is important. It is no longer appropriate to relegate elderly clients with cognitive impairment to the untreatable category of senile dementia. Additionally, there can be an overlap between depressive states and intellectual impairment in the elderly client.

Clients with the following findings are at the highest risk for organically induced psychological symptoms:

No previous psychiatric history
Signs and symptoms of medical illness
Unusual patterns of psychiatric symptoms
No prodromal phase
Absence of precipitating events

Table 3-6 lists some of the physical changes associated with the common medical problems known to cause psychiatric symptoms.[25,26]

TABLE 3-5   Organic Causes of Dementia/Delirium

I. Delirium/Reversible Dementia

Metabolic/hematologic
  Hyponatremia
  Severe anemia
  Hypokalemia
  Chronic obstructive pulmonary
    disease
  Hypo/hyperglycemia
  Cardiac arrhythmia
  Systemic lupus erythematosis
  Hepatic encephalopathy
  Elevated blood urea nitrogen

Endocrine
  Hypo/hyperthyroidism
  Hypo/hyperparathyroidism
  Addison's disease
  Cushing's disease

Neurological
  Transient ischemic attacks
  Subdural hematoma
  Stroke
  Normal pressure hydrocephalus
  Meningitis

Nutritional
  Vitamin B_{12} deficiency
  Pellagra
  Thiamine deficiency

Heavy metals
  Lead
  Arsenic

Drugs
  Digitalis
  Alcohol (delirium tremens)
  Cimetidine
  Benzodiazepines
  Barbiturates

Infections
  Pneumonia
  Upper respiratory infection
  Urinary tract infection

II. Nonreversible Dementia

Alzheimer's disease
Pick's disease
Huntington's chorea
Parkinson's disease
Multi-infarct dementia
Neurosyphilis
Creutzfeldt-Jakob disease
Cerebral malignancy

Questionably reversible
  Wernicke-Korsakoff's disease
  Long-standing myxedema
  Severe hypoxia/hypoglycemia

**TABLE 3-6   Physical Changes Associated with Organic/
Psychiatric Conditions**

Sleep/mood/energy changes
  Hypokalemia
  Hyponatremia
  Hypercalcemia
  Infections
  Anemia
  Hypoglycemia
  Hypothyroidism
  Mononucleosis
  Drugs: Benzodiazepines, pro-
    pranolol, neuroleptics, tricy-
    clic antidepressants, alcohol,
    antihypertensive agents

Skin/hair/weight changes
  Hypo/hyperthyroidism
  Cushing's disease
  Addison's disease
  Systemic lupus erythematosis
  Hepatitis/cirrhosis
  Drugs: steroids, anticholinergics,
    alcohol

Vital sign changes
  Hypo/hyperthyroidism
  Infections—all types
  Alcohol withdrawal
  Addison's disease
  Hypertension
  Anemia
  Diabetes mellitus
  Drugs: anticholinergic, digitalis,
    and tricyclic antidepressant
    toxicity; amphetamines

Gait/motor/sensory changes
  Neurosyphilis
  Wilson's disease
  Huntington's chorea
  Parkinson's disease
  Normal pressure hydrocephalus
  Cerebrovascular accident
  Multiple sclerosis
  Myasthenia gravis
  Wernicke-Korsakoff's syndrome
  Alzheimer's disease

Pupil/eye movement changes
  Wernicke-Korsokoff's disease
  Temporal lobe epilepsy
  Wilson's disease
  Neurosyphilis
  Drugs: PCP, marijuana, narcot-
    ics, overdose of barbiturates
    or benzodiazepines

Although many of the illnesses cause several physical changes, the list is a reminder of those areas easily assessed in the psychiatric emergency service.

Lastly, it is important to avoid single explanations for psychological problems. Clients with established psychiatric diagnoses may have *both* an exacerbation of psychiatric symptoms *and* a medical condition previously undiagnosed. The deinstitutionalized chronic psychiatric client is less able to provide a stable living environment and nutritious meals and to obtain satisfactory medical care. Thus, in addition to those clients with organically induced psychiatric symptoms, chronically mentally ill clients must also receive a medical screening.

Comparative Analysis of Clinical Data

In this section, the Assessment Model framework (Chapter 2) will be used as a guideline for comparing data representative of psychotic, organic, situational, and characterological problems. Data specific to each clinical problem will be presented for each step in the Assessment Model. These data are necessarily general and should not be construed as representative of all possible variations in the clinical presentations of these problems. Nonetheless, for purposes of decision making, generalizations are valuable in setting forth standards by which the clinician can determine reasons for the deviations found in actual clinical practice. This idea will be further developed in Chapter 9 when clinical problems, risk factors, and enabling factors are weighted in order to plan appropriate intervention strategies.

Many of the variations in the clinical presentation of the same psychiatric disorder are secondary to acute versus chronic phases of the disorder, client response to previous treatment versus refractory symptoms, and cooperation with versus resistance to therapy. These subcategories of assessment clarify the individual differences between clients with similar problems and between standard textbook descriptions and variations seen in clinical practice.

Assessment Model

Step One

Data collected by the first step of the Assessment Model are displayed in Figures 3-1, 3-2, and 3-3. These data are arranged according to the four clinical problems (situational, psychotic, characterological, and organic). Clients with situational or characterological problems vary little from the standardized norm on items of attire and physical appearance. There may be slightly more variation in clients with characterological dysfunctions secondary to their use of clothing as a means of conveying a particular message. Psychotic or organically impaired individuals will display marked variation in both dress and physical appearance, particularly when the problem is chronic. Acute psychotic episodes and sudden medical illnesses will not mask signs of previous good hygiene and health care, thus making this a useful marker for detecting organically induced problems.

Attire/Physical Appearance

Situational	Characterological	Psychotic	Organic
Hygiene and nutritional state are well maintained. Clothing is appropriate for age, sex, and occupational status. Variations are minimal, and occur secondary to level of distress, socio-economic, and cultural influences.	Hygiene and nutritional state are moderate to good. Clothing is representative of personality traits and self-image. Variations are moderate and secondary to the amount of decompensation and inability to attend to daily affairs.	Hygiene, health, and nutritional states are often compromised. Clothing choice is dependent on financial resources and mental capacity to attend to activities of daily living. Variations are marked, and represent diminished capacity to attend to personal and social standards of healthy adaptation.	Hygiene, health, and nutritional states are compromised. Dressing ability can also be compromised. Variations range from none to marked depending on the particular mental and physical deficits and the chronicity of the problem.
Examples	**Examples**	**Examples**	**Examples**
Clothing appropriate for age and sex Non-radical cultural affiliation	Eccentric choice of clothing	Disheveled, unkempt appearance Poor physical hygiene Eccentric choice of clothing Health status—moderate to poor	Disheveled Incomplete dress Poor health status and hygiene

Figure 3-1 Comparison of diagnostic data for attire/physical appearance.

69

Verbal Presentation/Emotional-Affective

Situational	Characterological	Psychotic	Organic
Organized, coherent description of the problem. Congruence between verbal content and affective state. Variation in content versus affect are secondary to emotional distress and unfamiliarity with the clinical setting.	Verbal content unclear, disjointed, and focused on symptomatology versus concrete events. Affective state incongruent with content: over or under reactive. Variation in clarity of content and affective response depend on personality style and level of distress.	Disorganized, incoherent presentation of problem. Content is bizarre and does not describe events clearly. Affective state is exaggerated secondary to psychotic process: depressed, irritable, euphoric, labile. Variation in verbal versus affective is low since both are usually equally disturbed.	Verbal presentation is impaired from disorganization and diminished clarity of thinking. Affective changes may not parallel verbal changes. Variation in verbal and affective states are marked, and may be congruent or incongruent depending on the particular disorder.
Examples	**Examples**	**Examples**	**Examples**
Clear content Emotional state matches content	Content is fairly clear Problem not readily identified Exaggerated affective state	Content is bizarre Ideas are unclear Speech is pressured or has long latencies Affect is depressed, euphoric, agitated or labile	Content is bizarre Signs of intellectual decline Affect blunted or incongruent with verbal presentation

Figure 3–2 Comparison of diagnostic data for verbal presentation/emotional-affective.

Eye Contact/Motor Behavior

Situational	Characterological	Psychotic	Organic
Eye contact and motor behavior are within the range of social norms. Variation from that may be secondary to tension, discomfort, depression, or social comfort.	Behavior is exaggerated from normal. Eye contact may be evasive or intense. Variation is secondary to the particular *type* of personality disorder.	Behavior is abnormally aggressive or psycho-motorically retarded. Eye contact is suggestive of: vigilance, hallucinatory experiences, autism.	Behavior is not goal directed. Variations range from aggressive, confused behavior to withdrawn, inactive states. Eye contact may be normal in degree, but lack registration of incoming event.
Examples	**Examples**	**Examples**	**Examples**
Socially shy Anxious Nervous Depressed Agitated	Acting-out Withdrawn Suspicious	Violent aggressive behavior Catatonic, withdrawn states Eye contact is fixed, staring, or distracted by psychotic experiences	Confused, wandering behavior Aggressive outbursts Behavior indicative of neurological dysfunction: paralysis, tremor, involuntary movement

Figure 3–3 Comparison of diagnostic data for eye contact/motor behavior.

71

Verbal/emotional presentations (Figure 3–2) have much the same pattern as the previous categories. That is, situational and characerological problems are less likely to distort the normal ability to communicate. The psychotic client tends to display evidence of disordered or delusional thinking, and the client with dementia or delirium may have impaired communication skills.

Eye contact/motor behavior (Figure 3–3) is again most disturbed in the psychotic or organically impaired client. Behavior will be distorted in the form of agitation or severe withdrawal. Motor and sensory changes may be apparent in the medically ill client (e.g., secondary to stroke, injury, or nutritional deficiencies). Pupil size and eye movements can alert the clinician to the conditions affecting these systems (see Table 3–6 for specific illnesses).

Step Two

The second phase of the Assessment Model uses selected MSE questions and a biological screening guide to refine further the hypothesis-generating process for the clinician. Figures 3–4, 3–5, and 3–6 display the findings from these items for each clinical problem.

Orientation and abstract reasoning (Figure 3–4) arc rarcly altered in the situationally or characterologically impaired client. The actual data may be incorrect in persons who have not had access to the usual routines which orient them (e.g., vacations, hospitalizations, and unemployment). Additionally, psychotic clients should be oriented, although their ability to perform tests of abstract reasoning may be limited secondary to concrete thinking or tangential, circumstantial thought processes. Obviously, this information is most useful in assessing clients with dementia or delirium who are unable to retain information and thus remain oriented.

Insight and judgment (Figure 3–5) are also impaired by psychotic and organic disorders. The client's ability to distinguish reality from psychotic experiences is diminished. And clients in the middle to late stages of dementia will be unable to judge their declining intellectual abilities. Judgment, insight, and abstract abilities should not be affected by situational or characterological problems, although baseline functions are dependent on education, intelligence, and cultural influences.

Figure 3–6 lists the types and phases of medical problems that mimic psychological problems. Many medical problems overlap the four clinical problems. Therefore, the differential diagnosis is dependent on the stage of the illness (e.g., acute, subclinical, or chronic) and the clinician's suspicion that an organic problem may exist.

Orientation/Abstractions

Situational	Characterological	Psychotic	Organic
Oriented to time, place, and person. Date may be incorrect secondary to changes in routine (unemployment). Abstract ability intact with variation secondary to educational, intellectual, or cultural influences.	Oriented to time, place, and person. Date may be incorrect secondary to changes in routine or preoccupation with self. Evaluation may be impaired secondary to poor cooperation. Abstraction ability impaired secondary to poor concentration and cooperation.	Oriented to time, place, and person. Testing difficult to perform secondary to psychotic thinking. Answers are usually bizarre, rather than wrong. Concrete thinking displayed in testing abstract abilities. Questions provoke evidence of thought disorder and rambling answers.	Disorientation to time and place, but person remains intact. Concreteness in tests of abstract reasoning. Declining intellectual abilities or decreased level of consciousness will prevent accurate responses.
Examples	**Examples**	**Examples**	**Examples**
Oriented x 3 Abstractions interpreted at level of common understanding	Oriented x 3 Abstractions consistent with intellectual, cultural, and educational opportunities Cooperation is the major impediment to testing	Distortions in sense of self and situation (delusional) Concrete interpretations of proverbs and similarities Bizarre, rambling answers	Delirium Dementia

Figure 3–4 Comparison of diagnostic data for orientation/abstractions.

Judgment/Insight

Situational

Good judgment in social/occupational roles. Insight dependent on level of psychological mindedness. Defense mechanisms structure access to psychological material.

Examples

Socially appropriate behavior.
Ability to understand the interaction between self and others in generating emotional conflict.

Characterological

Judgment and insight limited secondary to personality disorder type. Blurring of ego boundaries with others. Tendency to externalize blame.

Examples

Socially appropriate behavior constrained by dominant personality feature
Insight and judgment diminished by need to reduce anxiety

Psychotic

Portions of reality replaced with psychotic symptoms. Insight and judgment intact in those cognitive and perceptual experiences not affected by delusions, hallucinations and thought disorder.

Examples

Judgment impaired by self-image
Reality distorted to comply with psychotic symptoms

Organic

Judgment and insight impaired through psychotic symptoms or declining cognitive abilities.

Examples

Dementia with impaired cognitive processes
Organic psychosis with hallucinations and delusions

Figure 3–5 Comparison of diagnostic data for judgment/insight.

Biological Dysfunctions

Situational	Characterological	Psychotic	Organic
Illnesses/medications with an insidious onset which minimally affect cognition, mood, and social role functions. Clients may experience mild depression, fatigue, or anxiety.	Illnesses/medications which affect personality functions over time. Insidious onset or lengthy subclinical courses which gradually affect emotional stability. Clients may experience fatigue, irritability, apathy, and moderate depression.	Illnesses/medications which affect perceptual awareness, distort reality, diminish thinking processes, and exaggerate affective states. Psychotic symptoms may appear immediately in well functioning individuals; or occur only in the later stages of the illness. Coexistence with age-appropriate psychotic disorders makes diagnosis more difficult.	Illnesses/medications which affect cognitive processes and intellectual functions. These disorders mimic organic brain syndromes which are not reversible; and include the usual causes of delirium.
Examples	**Examples**	**Examples**	**Examples**
Anemia Diabetes Mellitus Subacute infections Drug reactions Chronic infections Early stages of endocrine, metabolic, or neurological problems which are difficult to diagnose (See Tables 3-3 and 3-4)	Epilepsy Organic brain syndrome Multiple sclerosis Myasthenia gravis Middle states of endocrine, metabolic, neurological, and infectious problems	See Tables 3-3 and 3-4	See Table 3-5

Figure 3–6 Comparison of diagnostic data for biological dysfunctions.

Step Three

The final phase in the Assessment Model differentiates the clinical problems on the basis of previous coping (Figure 3–7), duration of the problem and similarities to previous problems (Figure 3–8), and past medical and psychiatric history (Figures 3–9 and 3–10, respectively). These categories are most helpful in identifying established patterns of adjustment, particularly those affected by chronic psychotic problems and characterological disorders, and separate classic psychiatric disorders from organically induced psychological problems.

Previous coping abilities, the duration of the immediate problem, and similarities between past and current difficulties are useful in gauging the client's baseline level of functioning. Chronic psychotic, organic, and characterological problems are thus differentiated from situational crises and acute-onset organic disorders.

Lastly, a history of past psychiatric care shifts the assessment process toward differentiation between exacerbations requiring intensive treatment and situational crises which might be resolved in the psychiatric emergency service. The client's response to previous treatment further guides the planning for immediate treatment strategies. Similarly, the past medical history detects conditions/treatments likely to account for the psychiatric problem. Medications known to affect psychological parameters or recurring medical problems with psychiatric sequelae can be identified through this step.

Summary

Decision making requires the clinician to investigate several hypotheses throughout the data collection process. The reliability of the clinical diagnosis is dependent on the thoroughness of the data collected and the internal consistency of the signs and symptoms observed. This is particularly important in psychiatric care, in which individual items of data are rarely pathognomonic of a single disorder. Findings may overlap between disorders or may not exist within the same diagnostic category. Also, there can be great variability in the behavior of clients with the same clinical diagnosis.

The Assessment Model is designed to lead the clinician toward one or two general categories of psychiatric problems. Our intentions in using only general categories of psychiatric disorders are to broaden the evaluation process and to maintain several active hypotheses throughout the clinical interview. The attention to organic

Previous Coping Skills

Situational	Characterological	Psychotic	Organic
Evidence of good to excellent previous coping and emotional adjustment. Current situation is either catastrophic or unfamiliar.	Evidence of previous poor adjustment to social and interpersonal changes. Recurring themes/patterns of maladjustment.	Declining capacity to cope with new or threatening situations. Periods of remission will temporarily increase coping abilities.	Diminishing capabilities in clients with OBS. Others may return to previous level of adjustment once organic symptoms are controlled.
Examples	**Examples**	**Examples**	**Examples**

Mature Defenses:
  Sublimation
  Humor
  Suppression
Neurotic Defenses:
  Repression
  Intellectualization
  Reaction formation
  Identification
  Doing/undoing
  Displacement
  Isolation
Coping Style:
  Talks with others
  Tries out new behavior
  Continues to meet daily living requirements
	Neurotic Defenses:
	  See Column 1
	Primitive Defenses:
	  Dissociation
	  Regression
	  Distortion
	  Denial
	  Somatization
	  Splitting
	  Introjection
	Coping Style:
	  Regressive behavior
	  Problem avoidance
	  Externalize blame
	  Overwhelmed with emotional responses
		Primitive Defenses:
		  See Column II
		Evidence of depersonalization, derealization and psychotic distortion of reality
		Coping Style:
		  Retreats from active problem-solving
		  Vulnerable to changes in structure
			Defenses and coping style consistent with highest level of functioning
			Primitive Defenses:
			  Emerge secondary to psychotic symptoms or declining intellectual functions
			Coping Style:
			  Similarly deteriorates

Figure 3–7 Comparison of diagnostic data for previous coping skills.

77

Duration of Problem/Similarity to Previous Problems

Situational	Characterological	Psychotic	Organic
Problem may have existed for several months—days. Attempts to cope with the problem are evident. Similarities may exist in the form of anniversary reactions or themes of loss and threat to self-esteem.	Problem may be ongoing or fairly recent. Inability to cope with similar situations in the past. New threats easily threaten emotional stability. Themes of poor impulse control, frustration tolerance, and inability to delay gratification are present.	History of poor adjustment. Exacerbations of psychiatric symptoms during stressful times. Symptoms may appear quickly after threat occurs.	Recent onset of symptoms in individuals with acute illness. Previous poor coping in clients with established organic illness with deteriorating course.
Examples	**Examples**	**Examples**	**Examples**
Marital discord Family dysfunction Several deaths in family Financial/Academic problems	Changes in interpersonal relationships Therapist on vacation Employment role changes Illness in family	Changes in treatment plan Family system changes Alteration in daily routine	New situations overwhelm existing abilities If sufficiently ill will be unable to copy with daily events

Figure 3-8 Comparison of diagnostic data for duration of problem/similarity to previous problems.

Previous Medical History

Situational	Characterological	Psychotic	Organic
May have been in brief treatment or counseling in the past. Clients with established psychiatric diagnoses will be in treatment or achieved maximum benefit from past therapists.	May be in current treatment or had several therapists in the past. Possible hospitalization for suicide attempt/ideation. May have had several drug trials with psychopharmacologic agents.	Multiple hospitalizations and/or out-patient treatment. Previous/current psychopharmacologic treatment.	No previous psychiatric care, unless previous diagnosis of organic condition has been made. History may then mimic psychotic course.
Examples	**Examples**	**Examples**	**Examples**
Counseling from religious services or brief treatment No long-term medication use, or hospitalization	Multiple therapists/ hospitalizations Mixed diagnoses in past Various types of drugs used	Long-term treatment Multiple hospitalizations Medication use: Neuroleptic, anti-depressant, Lithium	Varies between no previous psychiatric treatment to multiple hospitalizations and drug use to control refractory symptoms.

Figure 3–9 Comparison of diagnostic data for previous medical history.

Previous Psychiatric History

Situational

No previous medical/surgical conditions or *chronic* illness requiring psychological adjustment to diminished *physical* capabilities.

Examples

Previous good health
Newly diagnosed medical problem which might require emotional adjustment

Characterological

Previous medical conditions which affect independence and lifestyle thus precipitating ineffective coping mechanisms. Otherwise no evidence of previous medical problems.

Examples

Previous good health
Chronic physical problem requiring major adjustment in lifestyle
Illnesses which affect mood and stress tolerance

Psychotic

No previous medical conditions which affect psychological processes.

Examples

Previous good health
Illness not likely to affect cognitive/emotional processes directly

Organic

Past medical, surgical, or traumatic injuries likely to affect psychological or cognitive processes directly. Drug use may also directly alter mentation and mood.

Examples

Established medical conditions known to affect emotional cognitive abilities
Illnesses with declining courses
See Tables 3-3, 3-4, 3-5

Figure 3-10 Comparison of diagnostic data for previous psychiatric history.

differentials is intended to broaden the psychiatric nurse's assessment skills to include more of a medical emphasis in psychiatric nursing care. Lastly, intervention planning is largely dependent on a constellation of both clinical findings and the client's psychological and social strengths and weaknesses. Thus, the Assessment Model also seeks to establish the level of premorbid adjustment and the previous health status as a means of predicting the most useful treatment setting.

References

1. Janis, I. L., and Mann, L.: *Decision Making: A Psychological Analysis of Conflict, Choice, and Commitment.* New York: Macmillan, 1977, p. 172.
2. Ibid., p. 206.
3. Udell, B., and Hornstra, R. K.: Hospitalization and presenting problems. *Comprehensive Psychiatry, 16,* 573–580, 1975.
4. Markin, R. A.: Information, decision-making, and the diagnostic process. *Comprehensive Psychiatry, 16,* 557–572, 1975.
5. Feigelson, E. B.; Davis, E.; Mackinnon, R.; Shands, H. C.; and Schwartz, C.: The decision to hospitalize. *American Journal of Psychiatry, 135,* 354–357, 1978.
6. Golan, N.: Using situational crises to ease transitions in the life cycle. *American Journal of Orthopsychiatry, 50,* 542–550, 1980.
7. Levinson, D.: *The Seasons of a Man's Life.* New York: Alfred A. Knopf, 1978.
8. Sheehy, G.: *Passages.* New York: Bantam Books, 1976.
9. Bellak, L., and Small, L.: *Emergency Psychotherapy and Brief Psychotherapy.* New York: Grune & Stratton, 1978, pp. 56-57.
10. Zonana, H.; Henisz, J.; and Levine, M.: Psychiatric emergency services a decade later. *Psychiatry in Medicine, 4,* 273–290, 1973.
11. Jacobson, G.: Personality disorders. In: Lazare, A. (ed.), *Outpatient Psychiatry: Diagnosis and Treatment.* Baltimore: Williams & Wilkins, 1979, pp. 419–439.
12. American Psychiatric Association: *Diagnostic and Statistical Manual of Mental Disorders,* 3rd ed. Washington, D.C., 1980, pp. 305–330.
12. Ibid.
13. Jacobson, G.: op. cit., pp. 419–420.
15. American Psychiatric Association., op. cit., p. 185.
16. Ibid., pp. 188–189.
17. Ibid., p. 215.

18. Ibid., p. 208.

19. Ibid., pp. 213–214.

20. Hall, R. C. W.: Medically induced psychiatric disease—An overview. In: Hall, R. C. W. (ed.), *Psychiatric Presentations of Medical Illness: Somatopsychic Disorders.* New York: Spectrum Publications, 1980, pp. 3–9.

21. Ibid., pp. 37–74.

22. Bassuk, E.; Schoonover, S.; and Gelenberg, A. (eds.): *The Practitioner's Guide to Psychoactive Drugs,* 2nd ed. New York: Plenum, 1983, pp. 9–13.

23. Pavkov, J.: *Clinical Assessment and Management of the Psychogeriatric Patient.* Spring House, Pa.: McNeil Pharmaceutical, 1983, pp. 1–12.

24. Boss, B.: The dementias. *Journal of Neurosurgical Nursing, 15,* 87–97, 1983.

25. Bates, B.: *A Guide to Physical Examination,* 3rd ed. Philadelphia: J. B. Lippincott, 1983.

26. Goroll, A.; May, L.; and Mulley, A: *Primary Care Medicine: Office Evaluation and Management of the Adult Patient.* Philadelphia, J. B. Lippincott, 1981.

ASSESSMENT OF SUICIDE

Chapters 4 and 5 will review current research and clinical practice in the areas of suicide and dangerousness. These aspects of client behavior have gained increased attention since involuntary commitment has been restricted to those mentally ill clients who pose a *significant* threat to themselves or others. In an effort to comply with the legal determinants of commitment, clinicians have attempted to define dangerousness and suicidal risk with greater precision.

Risk factors are clinically important, since suicide and homicide represent major sources of morbidity and mortality in psychiatric practice. Society has also relied on the mental health professional to protect them from clients whose deviant behavior represents a risk to others. This has become increasingly difficult since commitment laws have effectively increased the amount of deviance tolerated in the community in an effort to protect clients' rights.

The clinician's obligation in psychiatric emergency practice is the assessment of potential risk in clients with identifiable mental disorders. The amount of potential risk to clients and/or others will significantly affect intervention planning for these clients. Treatment settings provide varying degrees of restrictiveness, and the use of selected settings is dependent in large part on the need for a secure environment in which to provide care. Assessment of risk is one measure of the need for a secure environment versus a less restrictive setting, such as an outpatient clinic.

This chapter and Chapter 5 will review suicide and dangerousness, respectively. Case material will be presented to illustrate the variety of clinical forms of suicidal or dangerous behavior and the problem-solving process employed by the nurse clinician in planning care.

Evaluating clients' potential suicidal behavior is a difficult task for the clinician secondary to the severity of the consequences when an actual suicide attempt is successful. The goals of suicide assessment in emergency services should therefore focus on a thorough evaluation of the client's potential to attempt suicide and the institution of measures to protect the client from harm while psychiatric interventions are instituted.

In the absence of an attempted suicide, the clinician must rely on the client's self-reported suicidal intent. Distortions in the accuracy of data occur when the client minimizes symptoms to avoid interruption of a plan of involuntary hospitalization, or, conversely, exaggerates the intent to influence the behavior of another person, such as a family member or the clinician. Countertransferential distortions may also occur when the clinician has either a low or high tolerance for suicidal threats, resulting in unnecessary hospitalizations or a diminished response to clients, respectively.

Accompanying clinical data do not always increase the validity of clinical predictions about who is suicidal and how great is the risk of attempted suicide. The clinical characteristics and related antecedent events correlated with suicide are unfortunately widely represented in the general population. Although statistics show what age, gender, race, and marital status groups are highly represented among completed and attempted suicides, this knowledge is difficult to apply in each clinical situation.

A second difficulty is that those characteristics which are correlated with suicidal behavior, such as psychiatric diagnoses, lack specificity, making it difficult to establish to what degree they are useful predictors of suicidal behavior. For example, suicidal behavior may be correlated with depression, but not all patients who are depressed represent a serious suicide risk. Lastly, our ability to learn from our clinical experience is hampered by not knowing which clients we prevented from completing a suicide attempt or not understanding where we failed with those clients who completed suicide.

In spite of the theoretical constraints in predicting the actual potential for suicidal behavior in our clients, a thorough evaluation of such behavior is an essential component of psychiatric emergency care. Suicidal behavior may emerge during critical emotional times as a way of communicating distress to others, as the only alternative resource for problem solving, or as part of the symptomatology of psychotic thinking. The context in which the suicidal act has been conceived and the severity of the proposed attempt will assist the clinician in planning the intervention strategies most likely to reduce the overall risk to the client. The degree to which suicidal behavior will affect the treatment plan will of course depend on the balance of diagnostic factors, enabling factors, and treatment resources available to each client. These will be integrated into the later chapters of this book in the discussion of decision making in emergency care situations.

Clinical Content

The language used in the literature describing suicidal behavior has complicated the concept of suicide. Terms such as *suicidal thinking, suicidal gesture, suicide attempt,* and *severe depression* are often used interchangeably to denote suicide potential. The classification system of Beck and his associates has provided some clarity in the field of suicide research.[1] They have defined three major categories of suicide potential: completed suicides, attempted suicides, and suicidal ideation. Research instruments devised to measure the severity of suicidal behavior have relied on intentionality, lethality, mitigating circumstances, and method to determine the overall risk for each subject.[2-4] These instruments will be discussed in more detail in the section "Measurement Scales."

For the psychiatric emergency clinician, the most common clinical problems involve evaluation of the client who has made (and survived) a suicide attempt or is contemplating suicide as an alternative coping mechanism. The assessment process is probably best carried out through the use of an internal framework that defines the most pertinent areas under consideration. Figure 4–1 depicts the risk factors common to suicidal ideation and suicide attempt and categorizes the measures of severity specific to each behavioral category. The known risk factors for suicidal behavior are derived from specific demographic, diagnostic, and personality/behavior patterns significantly associated with suicide. Antecedent life events provide another dimension to the assessment process since these are the situations of sufficient magnitude to alter clients' coping mechanisms.

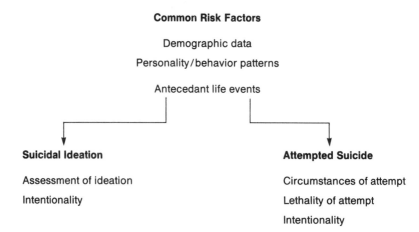

Figure 4–1 Categories for evaluating risk and severity of suicidal
behavior.

Common Risk Factors

There are six major demographic variables associated with a high incidence of suicide.[5-8] They are:

> Age: adolescence and 45 years or older
> Marital status: separated, divorced, or widowed
> Sex: male
> Race: white
> Living arrangement: living alone
> Employment status: unemployed

Diagnostic labels are useful in identifying those conditions commonly associated with suicidal symptomatology or likely to have suicidal behavior as part of the diagnostic criteria. Although the reliability of predicting suicidal behavior on the basis of the clinical
diagnosis is low, there are known psychiatric conditions which produce suicidal symptoms. The three most common ones are depression, alcoholism, and psychotic thinking. Suicidal ideation is one of
the criteria in the diagnosis of depression, according to DSM III.[9]
Alcoholism may intensify the underlying depressive state of an individual and reduce the client's impulse control when intoxicated.[10]
During psychotic episodes, clients may respond to their feelings of
worthlessness or carry out command hallucinations instructing them
to attempt suicide.

Personality and behavior patterns have their greatest impact on
the client's intentionality in contemplating suicide. Three character

traits identified by Tabachnick et al.[11] are likely to inhibit or facilitate self-destructive behavior: impulsivity versus efficacy of controls, rigidity versus flexibility, and isolation versus relatedness.

As a general rule, the more impulsive the individual, the greater the likelihood of self-destruction. Impulsive persons frequently do not consider the seriousness or the consequences of a suicidal act, and therefore do not possess mechanisms to control their behavior. The person with an impulsive personality style increases the risk to the self when the method of suicide is highly lethal or is carried out under the influence of alcohol.

The rigid personality style limits the client's alternatives in coping with stressful events. Regressive behaviors are likely to emerge during critical periods when the client is stressed and unable to perceive any solutions or alternatives for resolving the problem. Determining clients' rigidity may be difficult if they have been successful in many areas of their lives and decompensate only under severe stress; other clients are obviously more rigid, with a narrow life-style requiring relatively few coping mechnisms or creative alternatives in frustrating circumstances.

Evaluation of the client's isolation begins with a review of the demographic data. Social isolation may be secondary to a major change or loss in the client's life such as unemployment, death of a spouse, or retirement. The interaction of situational losses with developmental milestones may further intensify the perceived loss. In reviewing the demographic configuration, one must also note the pattern of the client's life-style, since individuals accustomed to isolation have usually adapted to that situation. During periods of crisis, it is important, however, to inquire about the client's ability to cope with the loss and the availability of important supportive resources. The convergence of loneliness, hopelessness, and despair may overwhelm even the most well-adjusted individual.

Although research studies have not focused directly on the correlation between personality factors and suicidal behavior, these concepts are clinically relevant from the perspective of reduced alternatives for coping with stressful events. The choice of suicide as a method for coping with stress is well recognized in those individuals with limited resources or few choices for solving problems. In the next section on antecedent life events, suicide emerges as a reasonable choice for some clients without acceptable alternatives. When this is combined with a rigid, impulsive, or isolated personality style, suicide is more likely to become an alternative coping mechanism.

Antecedent life events which are important in predicting suicidal behavior include previous suicide attempts, diminished social support systems, and recent or remote life changes. Previous suicide attempts, particularly those that were serious, or have occurred recently, and caused physical impairment, are strong indicators of future attempts.[12] A family history of suicide attempts is also an important factor in increasing the likelihood of suicidal behavior.[13]

The individual's support system plays an important part in deterring suicidal behavior. The social network can be called upon for additional support when the relationships are positive and seemingly responsive to the current problem. The risk is greater for persons with ambivalent, unavailable, or unresponsive (real or imagined) support systems.

Major losses commonly include loss of a spouse through death or divorce, unemployment or retirement, and physical illness. The elderly are particularly vulnerable to suicidal intent following major illness, malignant disease, or polysurgeries.[14] If these problems become entrenched and few options appear to resolve them, the risk increases in proportion to the futility of the situation.

The interaction of demographic characteristics, diagnostic category, personality/behavior patterns, and life events further guides the clinical evaluation of a given client's suicidal behavior. The psychiatric diagnosis is of primary importance, since "normal well" persons or those with only anxiety-related disorders will rarely attempt suicide even under the severest social stressors.[15] In the presence of social stressors, clients with diagnoses of alcoholism, conversion reactions, or antisocial character disorders are more likely to resort to suicide as an alternative coping mechanism. An even greater risk exists for clients with manic-depressive disorders or organic brain syndromes who may attempt suicide in the absence of social stressors, making the evaluation process complicated.

The high-risk factors discussed in this section are listed in Table 4–1.

Intentionality

The concept of *intentionality* provides a measurable index of the severity of both attempted suicide and suicidal ideation. Intentionality measures the lethality of the attempt (or plan) and the circumstances in which the suicide is contemplated. Specific measures address the client's expectations and attitudes about the plan, the amount of premeditation, precautions taken to avoid interruption, and efforts to communicate with others prior to the successful completion of the attempt.[16]

TABLE 4-1   High-Risk Factors Associated with Suicidal Behavior

Demographic factors
  Adolescence or 45 + years
  Male
  White
  Separated, divorced, or widowed
  Living alone
  Unemployed

Diagnostic factors
  Depression, particularly when severe, long-standing, and recently
    intensified
  Alcoholism
  Combination of depression and alcoholism
  Manic-depressive illness
  Organic brain syndrome

Antecedent events
  Previous attempts
    History of recent suicide attempts with serious intent
    Previous attempts that have not been successful in changing the
      behavior of persons close to the client
    Physical damage in conjunction with previous attempts
  Major changes
    Major losses (e.g., spouse, job, money)
    Major illness
    Medical conditions in an older person
    An escalation of long-standing problems with unavailable means for
      coping
  Support systems
    Unavailable, ambivalent, or unresponsive support system, or such a
      perception

Personality traits
  Impulsive character and behavior style
  Rigid style
  Isolative style

Expectations and attitudes refer to the lethality of the method
employed and the expectation that the method will be successful.
Premeditation deals with the final acts in anticipation of death, suicide, and active preparation for the attempt itself. *Precautions
against intervention* include the timing, location, and manner of the
suicide act to preclude interruption by others. *Communication with
others* addresses both unequivocal overt communication prior to the
attempt and actions to obtain help following the attempt. Each of
these items must be evaluated separately to determine the actual suicidal behavior of the client and the ideation with respect to each act.
    Correlations between intent and lethality are important in arriv-

ing at an index of the severity of the attempt or ideation. Both the client's perception of the lethality of the chosen method and his or her intention of carrying out the attempt in a way that avoids interruption determine the risk of completing the suicide act. Generally speaking, those clients with an accurate perception of the lethality of the method and a high intent would be at the greatest risk, while those with an accurate perception of its lethality and low intent would be at the lowest risk. Clients may, however, miscalculate the lethality of a method and even with low intent may make an unintentional yet successful suicide attempt.

Any discussion of intention must also include the motivational aspects of the client's suicidal behavior. The more consciously aware the client is of the effect of this behavior on another, the more likely it is to be an effort to communicate distress rather than an act of final, self-destruction. Conversely, the more the client is aware of the finality of a suicidal act, the more lethal and intentional it is. Assessment of the client's communication through suicidal behavior must focus both on the fact that a message is being delivered and on understanding the content of the message. Failure to receive the message may force the client to continue to engage in self-destructive behavior until an acceptable response occurs.

Measurement Scales

Three scales have been devised for research purposes in evaluating the severity or potential severity of suicidal behavior. Pierce's scale, shown in Table 4-2, measures the severity of suicidal behavior according to the circumstances of the attempt, the client's self-reported intent, and the risk of the method used.[17] There are 12 areas which are evaluated and scored from 0 to 2, depending on the severity of the behavior. As a general rule, the lethality of the attempt increases when the client has taken precautions against interruption, timed the attempt to avoid discovery, and made final arrangements such as leaving a suicide note, making a will, or taking out insurance. The client's self-report identifies his or her awareness of the lethality of the method, the wish to die, the amount of time spent contemplating the act, and the level of remorse at being unsuccessful. The clinician determines the overall risk of the attempt based on the client's knowledge of the lethality of the method and the seriousness of the method. Methods that leave little opportunity for reversal, such as firearms or jumping from high places, must be considered extremely serious.

TABLE 4–2   Intent Score Scale

Circumstances related to a suicide attempt

1. Isolation	0	Somebody present
	1	Somebody nearby or in contact (as by phone)
	2	No one nearby or in contact
2. Timing	0	timed so that intervention is probable
	1	Timed so that intervention is not likely
	2	Timed so that intervention is highly unlikely
3. Precautions against discovery and/or intervention	0	No precautions
	1	Passive precautions, e.g., avoiding others but doing nothing to prevent their intervention (alone in room, door unlocked)
	2	Active precautions, such as locking doors
4. Acting to gain help during or after the attempt	0	Notified potential helper regarding attempt
	1	Contacted but did not specifically notify potential helper regarding the attempt
	2	Did not contact or notify potential helper
5. Final acts in anticipation of death	0	None
	1	Partial preparation or ideation
	2	Definite plans made (e.g., changes in a will, taking out insurance)
6. Suicide note	0	Absence of note
	1	Note written but torn up
	2	Presence of note

Self-Report

1. Patient's statement of lethality	0	Thought that what he had done would not kill him
	1	Unsure whether what he had done would kill him
	2	Believed that what he had done would kill him
2. Stated intent	0	Did not want to die
	1	Uncertain or did not care if he lived or died
	2	Did want to die
3. Premeditation	0	Impulsive, no premeditation
	1	Considered act for less than one hour
	2	Considered act for less than one day
	3	Considered act for more than one day
4. Reaction to the act	0	Patient glad he has recovered

TABLE 4–2   continued

| | 1 | Patient uncertain whether he is glad or sorry |
| | 2 | Patient sorry he has recovered |

Risk

1. Predictable outcome in terms of lethality of patient's act and circumstances known to him	0	Survival uncertain
	1	Death unlikely
	2	Death likely or certain

2. Would death have occurred without medical treatment?	0	No
	1	Uncertain
	2	Yes

Source: D.W. Pierce: The predictive validation of a Suicidal Intent Scale: A five year follow-up. *British Journal of Psychiatry, 139*, 391–396, 1981.

A second scale developed by Beck and his associates measures the client's suicidal ideation.[18] The 19 items on the scale evaluate the cognitive and behavioral aspects of the suicide plan devised by the client (see Table 4–3). Again, the items are scored from 0 (lowest severity) to 2 (highest severity) and cover such factors as the wish to die, reasons for living, duration of suicidal ideation, attitudes toward suicide, method and expectation, and actual steps taken in the attempt.

The third scale, the Hopelessness Scale, was designed to measure the client's sense of futility versus optimism regarding future life events[19] (see Table 4–4). The "positive" items on the scale denote the hopeless percept of the client, while the "negative" items include the more optimistic outlook. Research studies using the Hopelessness Scale have confirmed the following hypotheses. First, depressed clients have an unrealistic, negative attitude toward the future, but these negative expectations recede when the depression lifts.[20] Second, the seriousness of the suicidal intent is more highly correlated with negative expectations than with depression. The statistical association between the suicidal intent and depression is an artifact resulting from joint attachment to a third variable—hopelessness.[21,22] Third, hopelessness has been shown to be covariate between drug abuse and suicidal intent.[23]

The Hopelessness Scale is designed to uncover the client's cognitive appraisal of future events and his or her motivation and drive to attain future goals. Those clients who view the future as bleak, without fulfilling experiences, and themselves as unable to change the course of events to their own satisfaction feel extremely hopeless and are at risk for suicide intent.

TABLE 4-3   Suicide Ideation Scale

1. Wish to live	0 1 2	Moderate to strong Weak None
2. Wish to die	0 1 2	None Weak Moderate to strong
3. Reasons for living/ dying	0 1 2	For living outweigh for dying About equal For dying outweigh for living
4. Desire to make active suicide attempt	0 1 2	None Weak Moderate to strong
5. Passive suicidal desire	0 1 2	Would take precautions to save life Would leave life/death to chance Would avoid steps necessary to save or maintain life
6. Time dimension: duration of suicide ideation/wish	0 1 2	Brief, fleeting periods Longer periods Continuous (chronic) or almost continuous
7. Time dimension: frequency of suicide	0 1	Rare, occasional Longer periods
	2	Persistent or continuous
8. Attitude toward ideation/wish	0 1 2	Rejecting Ambivalent, indifferent Accepting
9. Control over suicidal action/ acting-out wish	0 1 2	Has sense of control Unsure of control Has no sense of control
10. Deterrents to active attempt (e.g., family, religion, irreversibility)	0 1 2	Would not attempt because of a deterrent Some concern about deterrents Minimal or no concern about deterrents
11. Reason for contemplated attempt	0 1 2	To manipulate the environment: get attention, revenge Combination of 0 and 2 Escape, surcease, solve problems
12. Method: specificity/ planning of contemplated attempt	0 1 2	Not considered Considered, but details not worked out Details worked out/well formulated
13. Method: availability/ opportunity for	0 1	Method not available; no opportunity Method would take time/effort; opportunity not readily available

TABLE 4–3   continued

contemplated attempt	2a	Method and opportunity available
	2b	Future opportunity or availability of method anticipated
14. Sense of "capability" to carry out attempt	0	No courage, too weak, afraid, incompetent
	1	Unsure of courage, competence
	2	Sure of competence, courage
15. Expectancy/ anticipation of actual attempt	0	No
	1	Uncertain, not sure
	2	Yes
16. Actual preparation for contemplated attempt	0	None
	1	Partial (e.g., starting to collect pills)
	2	Complete (e.g., had pills, loaded gun)
17. Suicide note	0	None
	1	Started but not completed; only thought about
	2	Completed
18. Final acts in anticipation of death (e.g., insurance, will)	0	None
	1	Thought about or made some arrangements
	2	Made definite plans or completed arrangements
19. Deception/ concealment of contemplated suicide	0	Revealed ideas openly
	1	Held back on revealing
	2	Attempted to deceive, conceal, lie

Source: A.T. Beck; M. Kovacs; and A. Weissman: Assessment of suicidal intention: The Scale for Suicide Ideation. *Journal of Consulting and Clinical Psychology, 47,* 343–352, 1979.

Summary

Knowledge of the risk factors associated with suicidal behavior (e.g., suicidal ideation and attempted suicide) can assist the clinician in identifying those clients at high risk. Directly asking the client about suicidal ideation or previous attempts should be a fundamental part of the psychiatric interview. This is particularly important in psychiatric emergency care, in which the intensity of emotional conflict is often extremely high. The accompanying clinical data on support systems, psychiatric diagnosis, and the client's coping style further delineate the risk inherent in each situation.

The measurement scales for hopelessness, suicidal ideation, and suicidal intent provide specific areas of inquiry. These items can be directly assessed by asking the client the questions in each section. We do not suggest using a research format of obtaining a score for each client, but the accumulation of positive responses should alert the clinician to the severity of symptomatology present.

In the next section, we will describe the application of these tools in evaluating several clinical examples. The clinician's expertise in the evaluation of suicide will depend not only on knowledge of risk factors and suicidal symptomatology but also on the ability to synthesize the clinical material into a viable treatment plan that protects the client while simultaneously intervening with the precipitating problems.

TABLE 4-4   Hopelessness Scale

Positive Items

I might as well give up because I can't make things better for myself.
I can't imagine what my life would be like in 10 years.
My future seems dark to me.
I just don't get the breaks, and there's no reason to believe I will in the future.
All I can see ahead of me is unpleasantness rather than pleasantness.
I don't expect to get what I really want.
Things just don't work out the way I want them to.
I never get what I want, so it is foolish to want anything.
It's very unlikely that I will get any real satisfaction in the future.
The future seems vague and uncertain to me.
There's no use in really trying to get something I want because I probably won't get it.

Negative Items

I look forward to the future with hope and enthusiasm.
When things are going badly, I am helped by knowing they can't stay that way forever.
I have enough time to accomplish the things I most want to do.
In the future, I expect to succeed in what concerns me most.
I expect to get more of the good things in life than the average person.
My past experiences have prepared me well for my future.
When I look ahead to the future, I expect I will be happier than I am now.
I have great faith in the future.
I can look forward to more good times than bad.

Source: A.T. Beck; A. Weissman; D. Lester; and L. Trexler: The measurement of pessimism, the Hopelessness Scale. *Journal of Consulting and Clinical Psychology*, *42*, 861–865, 1974.

Clinical Application

Clients generally present with suicidal behavior in several ways. For some, suicidal ideation and intent may be the complaint and the reason for seeking care through the psychiatric emergency service. Others will have already attempted suicide, and either been found by others and brought in for care or changed their minds and voluntarily sought help. A third group may have other complaints such as depression or psychosis, but in the evaluation process the clinician discovers that suicidal ideation or intent is a major component of the problem.

Evaluation of the client's risk of suicidal behavior guides the clinician's intervention planning. Since psychiatric diagnosis is only one factor in determining the potential severity of the suicidal intent, the scales used to measure intent and lethality may be more useful. The constellation of factors which exist in each clinical situation will more directly guide the clinician's decision making in regard to treatment setting, use of supportive networks for the client, and suicide contracts for averting future attempts. A series of clinical examples will be used to demonstrate the variance in situations where suicidal ideation or attempts are the primary focus of psychiatric emergency care.

Clinical Example 4-1

The client is a 35-year-old single white male who had made a suicide attempt by cutting his wrists the day before he sought medical care in the emergency room. He was referred to the emergency psychiatric team after his wounds had been cleaned and dressed. On examination he was casually dressed, quiet, and did not appear to be in any distress. In a calm, unemotional way, he related the story of his suicide attempt. For several weeks he had been feeling hopeless and could not see any future for himself. He had left his post in a monastery because of fears that he was no longer suited to the priesthood. The previous day he had cut both wrists, hoping to bleed to death. When this proved unsuccessful, he went out for a walk. As he passed a gunsmith, it occurred to him that this sight was a message to kill himself with a gun. Having only limited funds, he purchased a rifle from a pawnshop and walked to the medical center complex to kill himself. His choice of setting was determined by his wish for his body to be donated to science. When the rifle misfired, he decided to seek medical care for his wrist wounds.

There is little question that the intentionality and lethality scores for this client would be quite high. The element of hopelessness is present, along with a persistent desire to die, few social supports, and access to lethal methods for carrying out his plan. Had the rifle not misfired, the client would have surely died. The personalization of environmental factors is also evidence of psychotic thinking. Whether or not the client would admit to further suicidal ideation, the risk of future suicidal behavior must be considered high in the absence of identifiable social stressors which might be quickly resolved. His lack of a supportive environment which would offer him safety mandates inpatient treatment.

The decision to admit clients who have attempted suicide is not always as clear as this clinical example indicates. Sometimes the clinical diagnosis, or lack of one, is a major impediment in determining the best course of action. This factor is particularly relevant when the client has been drinking or has characterological problems.

Clinical Example 4–2

The client is a 16-year-old female who took an overdose of aspirin the previous night. She was brought to the emergency room by her boyfriend after she told him what she had done. Medical treatment was instituted, and she remained in the emergency room overnight. On examination by the psychiatric clinician, the patient was sullen, refused to discuss her feelings about the overdose, and demanded to be released. It was learned that she was at a party the night before and was drinking alcohol. After an argument with her boyfriend, she went to the medicine cabinet and took a handful of aspirin. As she began to feel drowsy, she became frightened and asked for help. This is her first overdose, but she displays signs of impulsivity in her decision making and cannot recall why she intended to harm herself.

The *intent scale* is extremely useful in this clinical situation. The client would receive a relatively low score since there were mechanisms for rescue available, no premeditation, attempts made to secure help, and a low risk of lethality in the chosen method. The *suicidal ideation scale* would indicate only a slightly higher risk since the client was uncertain about the lethality of the method, was upset and intoxicated at the time of the attempt, and may be ambivalent about the situation which precipitated it. The perceived danger in this situation is the age of the client, her choice of suicide to solve an interpersonal conflict, and her lack of knowledge about the possible risk of the method chosen. Her impulsivity places her at high risk for accidentally succeeding during any future attempt.

Attempts to discuss the situation with psychiatric personnel are similarly reduced by her withdrawn, angry stance. Hospitalizing this client against her will may make the clinician feel more secure but might further alienate the client. Legal grounds for involuntary admission are minimal in the absence of a psychiatric illness and stated future plans to harm herself.

Interventions by emergency psychiatric personnel might realistically focus on mobilization of her support system and attempts to engage her in some immediate problem solving about her coping methods. Questions about how she handles frustrating events in her life, recent problems which have overwhelmed her, and significant persons in her life whom she would call on for assistance could begin the task of uncovering her potential ability to learn from the suicide attempt. It is hoped that avoidance of a punishing attitude by the clinican will reduce her antagonism toward psychiatric personnel. Adolescent clients are at risk for suicidal behavior and have an inability to discuss many threatening events in their lives. When cooperation is limited, the family may need to provide the element of safety for the client. Efforts should be directed toward helping the family understand the risk of suicide as well as the need to support the client and understand his or her problems. If the suicide attempt has been a culmination of ongoing problems, the family might secure treatment for the client or engage in family treatment until changes occur.

Perhaps the most complicated clinical situations seen in the psychiatric emergency service with respect to suicidal ideation or attempts are those involving clients who are chronically suicidal, have made previous attempts, and have borderline characterological traits or disorders. These clients are at high risk for lethal suicide attempts during periods of psychological decompensation. When the client is unknown to the emergency room personnel, the absence of a previous psychiatric history makes prediction of future behavior limited.

Clinical Example 4–3

The client is a 30-year-old white single female who was brought in for treatment by ambulance after calling the local crisis telephone service and threatening to harm herself. Workers became concerned by her persistent refusal to give an address or name. Examination by the psychiatric clinician revealed that the client is a nurse and has been in therapy for several years with various local therapists. Her history reveals several suicide attempts, usually during periods of decompensation and emotional turmoil in her life. She has been diagnosed in the past as having a borderline personality disorder, but is relatively functional in terms of maintaining employment and contact with her therapist.

Approaches to this type of client often vary with the philosophical orientation of the clinician, who may have greater or lesser tolerance of chronic suicidal behavior. It is obviously impractical for such a client to remain hospitalized for life. However, it is the responsibility of the clinician to protect the client from further harm. Collaboration with the outpatient therapist currently treating the client provides the emergency room staff with data on previous suicide attempts and current stressors in the client's life which may have provoked the current episode.

This client's occupation as a nurse may increase the lethality of a suicide attempt since it is likely that she would know which methods are most fatal. Additionally, her failure to contact her therapist during the recent crisis might suggest a greater inability to work through the problem. The long-term treatment of this client will probably include a series of suicide attempts or threats during crises. The role of the psychiatric emergency service must remain limited and confined to the current episode. Fears of reinforcing suicidal behavior should not dictate treatment planning that would place the client at risk for further harm during the immediate crisis.

Alternatives for caring for the client without hospitalizing her include the use of a holding bed area, contacting her therapist to determine what other alternatives exist to ensure her safety for the evening, or planning for a limited admission until she becomes psychologically stable. Avoiding a power struggle with these clients is invaluable in averting further behavior aimed at meeting their dependency needs. Efforts which minimize their distress are often met with increased suicidal behavior in an attempt to make their suffering known to the care provider.

Summary

Suicidal behavior, defined as suicidal ideation or suicide attempts, is a common clinical problem in the psychiatric emergency service. Assessment of the intentionality, severity, and potential lethality of the client's suicidal behavior is a critical task for the clinician. Research tools designed to measure suicidal ideation, hopelessness, and suicide intention have great clinical usefulness in assessing the risk for completed suicide in psychiatric clients. Although these tools are not helpful in arriving at a score which would dictate clinical interventions, they can provide the clinician with an overall impression of the inherent risk.

When these tools are used in combination with psychiatric diagnosis, current life events, personality factors, and demographic profiles of suicidal clients, they can structure care planning in a safe, humanistic way. The clinician's clinical judgment must rely on valid assessment tools as well as the constellation of clinical factors in each situation.

Clients who are diagnosed as having clinical problems of depression, psychosis, manic-depressive illness, or organic brain syndrome are likely to have an increased potential for suicidal behavior. In the absence of stated suicidal feelings, clinicians should address the potential for suicidal behavior during their evaluations. Similarly, the client who is intoxicated has a diminished capacity to assess the lethality of a suicide attempt and may experience increased dysphoria under the influence of alcohol.

References

1. Beck, A. T.; Beck, R.; and Kovacs, M.: Classification of suicidal behaviors: I. Quantifying intent and medical lethality. *American Journal of Psychiatry, 132,* 285–287, 1975.
2. Beck, A. T.; Davis, J. H.; Frederick, C. J.; et al.: Classification and nomenclature. In: Resnik, H., and Hathorn, B. (eds.), *Suicide Preven-*

tion in the Seventies. Washington, D.C., Government Printing Office, 1973, pp. 7–12.

3. Beck, A. T.; Kovacs, M.; and Weissman, A.: Assessment of suicidal intention: The Scale for Suicide Ideation. *Journal of Consulting and Clinical Psychology, 47,* 343–352, 1979.

4. Pierce, D. W.: The predictive validation of a Suicidal Intent Scale: A five year follow-up. *British Journal of Psychiatry, 139,* 391–396, 1981.

5. Tuckman, J., and Youngman, W. F.: A scale for assessing suicide risk of attempted suicides. *Journal of Clinical Psychology, 24,* 17–19, 1968.

6. Papa, L. L.: Responses to life events as predictors of suicidal behavior. *Nursing Research, 29,* 362–369, 1980.

7. Beck, A. T.; Weissman, A.; Lester, D.; and Trexler, L.: The measurement of pessimism, the Hopelessness Scale. *Journal of Consulting and Clinical Psychology, 42,* 861–865, 1974.

8. Holinger, P. C., and Offer, D.: Prediction of adolescent suicide: A population model. *American Journal of Psychiatry, 139,* 302–307, 1982.

9. American Psychiatric Association: *Diagnostic and Statistical Manual of Mental Disorders,* 3rd ed. Washington, D.C., 1980.

10. DiVasto, P. V.; West, D. A.; and Christy, J. E.: A framework for the emergency evaluation of the suicidal patient. *Journal of Psychiatric Nursing and Mental Health Services, 17,* 15–20, 1979.

11. Tabachnick, N. D., and Farberow, N. L.: Assessment of self-destructive potentiality. In: Beck, A. T.; Resnik, H. L. P.; and Letteri, D. J. (eds.), *The Prediction of Suicide.* Bowie, Md., Charles Press, 1974, pp. 60–77.

12. Sletten, I. W., and Barton, J. L.: Suicidal patients in the emergency room: A guide for evaluation and disposition. *Hospital and Community Psychiatry, 30,* 407–411, 1969.

13. Woodruff, R. A.; Clayton, P. J.; and Guze, S. B.: Suicide attempts and psychiatric diagnoses. *Diseases of the Nervous System, 33,* 617–621, 1972.

14. Litman, R. E., and Farberow, N. L.: Emergency evaluation of self-destructive potentiality. In: Beck, A. T.; Resnik, H. L. P.; and Letteri, D. J. (eds.), *The Prediction of Suicide.* Bowie, Md., Charles Press, 1974, pp. 48–59

15. Robins, E.; Schmidt, E. H.; and O'Neal, P.: Some interrelations of social factors and clinical diagnoses in attempted suicide: A study of 109 patients. *American Journal of Psychiatry, 114,* 221–231, 1957.

16. Beck, A. T.; Weissman, A.; Lester, D.; and Trexler, L.: Classification of suicidal behaviors. *Archives of General Psychiatry, 33,* 835–837, 1976.

17. Pierce, D. W.: The predictive validation of a Suicidal Intent Scale: A five year follow-up. *British Journal of Psychiatry, 139,* 391–396, 1981.

18. Beck, A. T.; Kovacs, M.; and Weissman, A.: Assessment of suicidal intention: The Scale for Suicide Ideation. *Journal of Consulting and Clinical Psychology, 47,* 343–352., 1979.

19. Beck, A. T.; Kovacs, M.; and Weissman, A.: Hopelessness and suicidal behavior: An overview. *Journal of the American Medical Association, 234,* 1146–1149; 1975.

20. Vatz, K.; Winig, H.; and Beck, A. T.: *Pessimism and a sense of future time construction as cognitive distortions in depression.* Unpublished manuscript, University of Pennsylvania Medical School, 1969.

21. Minkoff, K.; Bergman, E.; Beck, A. T.; and Beck, R.: Hopelessness, depression, and attempted suicide. *American Journal of Psychiatry, 130,* 445–459, 1973.

22. Beck, A. T.; Kovacs, M.; and Weissman, A., op. cit.

23. Weissman, A. N.; Beck, A. T.; and Kovacs, M.: Drug abuse, hopelessness, and suicidal behavior. *The International Journal of the Addictions, 14,* 451–464, 1979.

CHAPTER 5

ASSESSMENT OF DANGEROUSNESS/ VIOLENCE

Assessment of dangerous behavior in the mentally ill has become an increasingly important aspect of psychiatric emergency care since many states have included it as one of the three criteria (dangerousness to oneself and inability to care for oneself being the other two) for involuntary confinement. This has effectively limited the power of the psychiatric profession to commit individuals who are mentally ill but not dangerous to themselves or others. Nonetheless, there remains a significant responsibility for the mental health professional to identify potentially dangerous individuals and protect society from their violent acts. Since assessment of dangerousness is relatively new in clinical practice, there has been a tendency for clinicians to overestimate the violent potential in the mentally ill population.

This tendency stems from a lack of experience in researching and classifying dangerous behavior and the fear engendered in clinicians when a client commits a violent act. Without clear evaluation criteria, the clinician often relies on an emotional response to arrive at a clinical decision. As Scott notes, "The dangerous individual is simply one who engenders too much anxiety."[1]

In addition to the lack of clarity in assessing dangerous behavior, the psychiatric profession is now forced to interface with the legal system in judging the client's capacity for violent behavior. Psychiatric clinicians are frequently asked to determine if the client is dangerous secondary to mental illness and should be hospitalized, or whether the client should be treated as a criminal offender and have the consequences determined by the legal system. The existing lack of clarity in establishing psychiatric diagnoses further complicates the client's status as criminal versus patient. This is particularly true with respect to the recent debate over the ''not guilty by reason of insanity'' status now afforded some mentally ill persons in the legal system. This issue will be discussed more fully later in this chapter with respect to the sentencing mechanisms for criminal offenders versus the open-ended terms of confinement for the mentally ill.

Clinicians may also overpredict dangerousness in clients since the burden of responsibility rests more with them than with the client. Existing data indicate that violence may be more egosyntonic when associated with lower socioeconomic status, exposure to violence during the child-rearing years, drug and alcohol use, and provocative precipitating events.[2,3] The use of violence in these situations is more likely to be perceived as acceptable by the client and not indicative of emotional instability requiring psychiatric care.

Although there are multiple barriers to the accurate assessment of dangerousness and/or violence in the psychiatric emergency room population, there is a clinical obligation to identify potentially violent individuals. This chapter will present an overview of current research in predicting violent behavior and the variables commonly associated with violent acts. An additional discussion will focus on victims of abuse, namely, battered wives, rape victims, children, and the elderly. Methods for identifying abused individuals and planning intervention strategies to protect these clients from further harm will be discussed. Lastly, clinical examples will be presented to illustrate various clinical manifestations of dangerous behavior.

Clinical Content

Overview of Research Findings

Violence has been documented in the history of humanity throughout the centuries, and it is doubtful that it will be totally eradicated in the near future. It is important, however, that we understand who may commit acts of violence in the hope of thwarting their untoward effects and planning appropriate interventions to reduce the potential for violence in our society. One of the prime considerations in our legal and mental health care system today is the prediction of who will commit a violent act under which set of circumstances.[4]

The role of the psychiatric emergency clinician in assessing dangerousness is twofold. First is the accurate identification of individuals who represent a threat to society secondary to violent acts arising from a disturbed mental state. These violence-prone individuals are likely to commit dangerous acts only under conditions of extreme emotional instability; once stabilized through psychiatric care, they return to a less violent state. Examples include clients who are demented, delirious, psychotically depressed, acutely psychotic, or withdrawing from drug/alcohol addiction. The dangerousness of these individuals is secondary to attempts to protect themselves because they misperceive others' motives and become frightened or confused. Once their mental state is returned to normal, their potential for violence approximates their lifetime risk, as noted in Table 5–1.

The second role of the psychiatric emergency clinician is the

TABLE 5–1   Short-Term versus Long-Term Predictors of Violence

	SHORT TERM *(24 hours to 1 week)*	LONG TERM *(lifetime potential)*
Age	15–30 years of age	Variable
Sex	Male	Either, although males more prone than females
Race/culture	Disadvantaged populations	Same
Diagnostic categories	*Organic:* Acute Organic Brain Syndrome Temporal lobe epilepsy Pathological intoxication	*Organic:* Delirium Dementia Temporal lobe epilepsy Minimal brain dysfunction Severe depression
	Psychotic: Paranoid Acute psychotic	
	Personality Disorder: Antisocial Borderline Passive-aggressive	*Personality Disorder:* Antisocial Explosive Borderline Passive-aggressive

TABLE 5–1   continued

	SHORT TERM *(24 hours to 1 week)*	LONG TERM *(lifetime potential)*
	Drugs/alcohol: Abuse/intoxication Withdrawal	*Drugs/alcohol:* Amphetamines Cocaine Phencyclidine Methylphenidate
Precipitating event	Meaningful provocation Loss of usual control mechanisms	Drug/alcohol use Significant provocation
Environmental factors	Volatile situations Highly stressful events	Disadvantaged urban dwelling Poor access to educational/ vocational resources
Associated factors	Recent violent act History of previous violence Verbal threat	High level of frustration Family violence Peer pressure Availability of weapons and alcohol
Behavioral clues	Tension Speech tone/strength of voice Agitation/pacing	Chronically out of control Long suffering/over-controlled behavior

identification of those individuals who have a high potential for violence over a long-term period and may or may not be dangerous in the near future. This group is composed of individuals with personality disorders, chronic psychotic states, and drug/alcohol abuse. In these clients, violence is more often precipitated by events that are psychodynamically meaningful or coincide with existing distortions of reality. The reality distortion may be a psychotic state or may merely reinforce existing perceptions of abandonment, neglect, or rejection by important figures in their lives. Psychiatric treatment for these individuals may restore greater personal control over time. These clients may be the ones who account for the high rates of over-prediction of violence. Although they seem to be at risk for violent behavior, they may never encounter the circumstances necessary to cause them to lose control and become dangerous.

   Much of the research on violence has utilized both the criminally insane and mentally ill populations to predict future episodes of violence. Rates of overprediction of future violence in the criminally insane population range from 30 to 95%.[5-7] One study of criminally insane offenders found that for every accurate prediction of future violence, there were 326 incorrect ones, and another study noted that for every 100 persons classified as dangerous, no more than a third engaged in subsequent violence. Although criminal offenders are accorded protection through the legal system and prescribed terms of confinement for a given infraction, the legal safeguards for the mentally ill are only beginning to emerge.[8]

Although the legal system currently attempts to define the relationship between criminal acts, mental illness, and sentencing procedures, there continues to be arbitrary application of civil and legal restrictions. When the seriousness of the violent act requires legal charges, the mentally ill offender is more likely to come under the legal system. If, however, the offense is less serious, action is dependent on the mental health and legal resources available in the community. Thus, the coexistence of criminal behavior and mental illness allows the client access to either the mental health care system or the criminal system.

The mentally ill are not, however, the most dangerous group when compared with criminal offenders.[9] Although schizophrenics are considered the most dangerous group, diagnostically, in the mentally ill population, their rate of violent acts is low—5 in 10,000.[10] Similarly, in terms of assaultive behavior on inpatient units, the paranoid schizophrenic is more likely to be assaultive, but there is no difference between voluntarily and involuntarily admitted clients in terms of their potential for violence.[11] Lastly, rates of violence are no higher for the mentally ill population than for the community at large.[12]

The literature is therefore inconclusive regarding the association between violence and mental illness, except to note strong patterns of overprediction in the mentally ill group. Therefore, mental illness should be *one* factor in determining potential dangerousness, not *the* factor, as it has been. It is unfortunate that the concept of dangerousness to others became one of the criteria for involuntary confinement of the mentally ill before clinical practice/research had defined it more precisely. Nonetheless, in spite of the overprediction of violence in the mentally ill population, there remains a commitment to provide treatment in the least restrictive setting and to protect the rights of clients in the process of receiving care. Currently, the goals are to understand dangerous behavior better and to improve assessment methods.

Predictors of Violence: Short Term

In an attempt to improve the prediction of dangerous behavior in the mentally ill population, attention is being placed on short-term predictions.[13] Short-term predictors attempt to identify the potential for violent behavior within 24 hours to one week. This is the usual amount of time allowed by many states for the detainment of dangerous, mentally ill individuals prior to a court hearing. This time is often sufficient for the client to be removed from a stressful situation and regain personal control. Otherwise, it allows care providers an opportunity to evaluate further clients requiring additional interventions. In any event, short-term detention in mental health facilities quickly transfers the responsibility for longer-term confinement of dangerous individuals to the jurisdiction of the courts, where some believe it belongs.[14,15]

Further support for using short-term predictors comes from studies of newly admitted inpatients. One study noted that most incidents of violence occurred within the first 10 days in both committed and noncommitted clients.[16] It was also found that after 20 days of hospitalization, clients labeled dangerous were no more assaultive than other clients. In this study, the most accurate predictors of violence were a previous history of violence or a physician's assessment of potential danger.

Some of the diagnostic and behavioral variables associated with dangerousness in the emergency room are listed in Table 5-1 under short-term predictors.[17] The diagnostic categories consist of those conditions known to alter neurological functions (e.g., organic conditions) or diminish personal control (e.g., drug/alcohol use, acute psychosis, and personality disorders).

Additional short-term predictors associated with violence include age (15–30 years old), male gender, a previous history of violence, and a history of drug and alcohol abuse.[18-20]

Prior to generating a profile of the client most likely to be considered dangerous, it is important to cite another definition of dangerousness: "The concept of violence is a semantic labyrinth, a term used at times for polemical ends rather than for exact meaning. Violence may exist primarily in the eyes of the beholder, and its boundaries are extraordinarily complicated to pinpoint."[21] With this in mind, the persons (perhaps) most associated with immediate violence are predicted to be of male gender, ages 15–30, diagnosed with a personality disorder, acute psychosis, or an organic mental condition, a previous history of violence, and threatening behavioral mannerisms. Since violence is often a learned behavior, clients raised in abusive, volatile situations, or currently having such a life-style, might also engage in violence.

The value of identifying short-term predictors of dangerousness in the mentally ill population is that it narrows the variables to those most highly associated with immediate acts of violence. This effectively curbs the clinician's tendency to estimate dangerousness in anything more than the immediate future. It may also reduce the clinician's resonsibility for predicting longitudinal behavior in clients whose risk for violence is no greater than that of the general population.

Predictors of Violence: Long Term

As noted earlier, prediction of violence over a long-term period has been highly inaccurate, particularly in identifying many false positives. In an attempt to understand better the meaning of and potential for violence in our society, the biopsychosocial factors associated with violence will be reviewed.[22]

Patterns of violence are not uniform across individuals. Some persons may be chronically out of control, whereas others manifest only a rare outburst of violence. The chronically uncontrolled individual will be easily stimulated to violence, whereas the long-suffering, overcontrolled individual may erupt unexpectedly. The following psychosocial factors have specific relationships with violent behavior and may guide the clinician in determining the long-range risk for dangerousness.

1. Sociological factors: Most individuals who commit violent acts are disadvantaged, urban-dwelling young males.[23] These individuals are likely to use violence as a means of reducing frustration and gaining better access to rewards of society commonly obtained through vocational/educational opportunities.

2. Environmental factors
   a. Family: Family members may be the victims of crime or may use violent methods to obtain gratification.
   b. Peer environment: Peers may encourage violent behavior.
   c. Job environment: Access to a satisfactory job is correlated with successful rehabilitation and success during parole.[24]
   d. Availability of victims, weapons, and alcohol: All three factors are related to an increased likelihood of violence.[25]

3. Developmental factors: The family environment in which the individual was raised may shape later behavior. An atmosphere of turbulence, inconsistent discipline that was perceived as punitive, and child abuse can lead to aggressive tendencies in adulthood.[26]

4. Psychiatric diagnosis: Some generalizations can be made about those conditions likely to diminish the client's capacity for self-control.

      a. Organic brain syndrome, dementia, and delirium may cause the person to become paranoid and frightened.

      b. Seriously depressed clients may become irritable and delusional, and may seek to harm their family and themselves to protect themselves from unforeseen events.[27]

      c. Personality disorders account for some of the most seriously violent behavior demonstrating antisocial and explosive tendencies.

5. Biological factors: These are related to some of the organic brain syndromes since neurological impairment or drug effects may diminish personal control. Minimally brain-damaged children may become more violent as adults, and temporal lobe epilepsy may alter one's capacity for impulse control.[28,29]

6. Extrinsic factors: Drug and alcohol abuse are frequently associated with violence and poor impulse control.[30] Central nervous system stimulants, amphetamines, cocaine, phencyclidine, and methylphenidate are more likely to precipitate violence, whereas marijuana and heroin are less likely to have this effect.

These factors provide a range of alternative psychosocial explanations for violent behavior. (See Table 5-1). The difficulty in using them to predict clinical behavior in clients is that not all individuals exposed to these situations are considered dangerous. Nor is there any clear demarcation between the types of behaviors labeled dangerous for these individuals. As noted earlier, the arousal of fear in the clinician, family member, or bystander is not sufficient to label the client dangerous.

Criminal offenders may more appropriately display some of the long-range characteristics associated with dangerousness. In a study comparing a control group of offenders with a group convicted of murder, the following factors emerged more often for the offenders convicted of murder: a preponderance of personality disorders; childhood symptoms of enuresis, hyperactivity, nail biting, fighting, and tantrums; and a family environment characterized by violence, marital separation, poor relationships with parents, and low evaluation of the individuals by their fathers.[31]

Assessment Methods

The assessment of the client's potential for violence is hindered by the unpredictable nature of dangerous behavior and the client's unwillingness to identify violence as a problem. Although some clients approach the psychiatric emergency service requesting help for their violent tendencies, more often violence is either egosyntonic or used to protect the client against real or imagined harm.

In order to identify the potential for violence in clients, an indirect assessment style may be more effective.[32] Figure 5–1 suggests some of the parameters of a nondirective interview. Without approaching the topic directly, to avoid denial, the clinician notes the circumstances that elicit aggression and the steps the client uses to integrate/resolve the experience. Identifying these factors in each case alerts the clinician to the possibility of continued stress in the client's life and the internal mechanisms for maintaining self-control. As noted in the diagram, the precipitating stress may represent a conscious or unconscious provocation. Thus, in addition to identifying the obvious stressor, the clinician must seek to understand the psychodynamic meaning of the event. The way in which the client internalizes the event is also a useful measure of egosyntonic affiliation with violent/aggressive behavior.

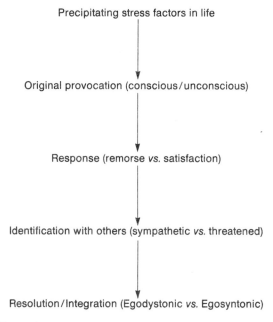

Precipitating stress factors in life

Original provocation (conscious/unconscious)

Response (remorse *vs.* satisfaction)

Identification with others (sympathetic *vs.* threatened)

Resolution/Integration (Egodystonic *vs.* Egosyntonic)

Figure 5–1   Interview format for violence assessment.

A more directed assessment of violence seeks to understand the particulars of the episode. Table 5–2 is a composite of Rada's[33] systematic assessment method and Geis'[34] framework for assessing the five dimensions of violence (Table 5–2, Part III). The phases of the violent episode—preassault, assault, and postassault—identify the severity and consequences of the act. Here the clinician is able to establish how likely the event is to recur and what intervention measures might avert future episodes.

Part II of Table 5–2 lists those conditions known to reduce self-control or distort reality and increase the client's sense of vulnerability. Lastly, Part III further describes the violent situation and offers some guidelines for predicting future violence. For example, do the circumstances that were present during the previous episode still exist? Has the client gained any measure of self-control to avoid the use of violence in another provocative situation?

Violence does require provocation that is meaningful to the individual, as well as a lack of morality, reality testing, or self-control which allows the provoked individual to see nothing wrong with the act or be unable to exercise self-control in time.[35] Slaby notes that violence is caused more frequently by persons who have a number of prior arrests, have a previous history of a severe offense, are impulsive and stimulus seeking, and live in a subculture of stress and violence.[36] Further, violence is often directed toward family members or close personal acquaintances.

TABLE 5–2 Assessment of Violence

  I. Phases of assessing assaultive behavior
    A. Preassault phase: issues of provocation
    B. Assault phase: directed to person/place versus random act
    C. Postassault phase: response of the client following the assault

  II. Determinants of the assaultive act
    A. Situational: dynamic cause of anger/fear from dependency/ rejection
    B. Organic: temporal lobe epilepsy, electrolyte imbalance, organic brain syndrome
    C. Psychotic: distorted perception of events
    D. Drug/Alcohol: disinhibition/loss of control

  III. Dimensions of violence
    A. Who is the recipient of violence?
    B. Where does it occur?
    C. When does it occur?
    D. What is its form?
    E. Why did it occur?

Victims of Abuse

Women are commonly victims of abuse within the family. It is estimated that in as many as 50% of American families there is some degree of abuse.[37] Studies of abused wives note that up to 84% require medical treatment secondary to these episodes.[38] The number of wives abused annually is in the range of 5 to 6 million.[39] Most cases of abuse are likely to occur early in the marriage, and some 25% of the victims were abused prior to marriage.[40,41]

Children are frequently the victims of abuse through excessive disciplinary action by parents or sexual abuse. Rates of incest are estimated at 5,000 per million.[42] These rates are even higher among psychiatric populations. The most common abuser in cases of incest is the father or stepfather.[43]

The elderly are another group likely to be victims of abuse. This is a relatively new phenomenon (or the reporting of it is new), so little is known about its prevalence. White females who live alone or with relatives are the most frequent victims.[44] Violence toward these individuals comes from other relatives or caregivers.

Rape victims are another group likely to be seen in the emergency service, and may require the assistance of psychiatric personnel. Rape, of course, is a criminal offense, but nonetheless is treated in a variety of ways by the legal system and the victim herself. Although victims' rights are being protected more today, there is still a great deal of stigma associated with rape. Women still retain the option of not reporting rape. This trend will undoubtedly continue until there is less emphasis on the victim as provoker.

Characteristics of Victims

One common factor linking victims of abuse, regardless of their age or gender, is that they often hide the fact of abuse, and when they do come forth they may not be believed. Battered wives are often reluctant to discuss how they were injured. Similarly, elderly victims may fear further harm if they disclose the incident, particularly when they are vulnerable and helpless to prevent further abuse. This same situation applies to children, who are unable to remove themselves from the abusive environment or provide for their own needs without adult assistance.

The types of injuries inflicted on victims is also similar. Injuries are usually to the head, neck, and trunk in both children and abused wives. It is also common to find old, healing injuries in these individuals, indicating past violent episodes. The client may not readily admit that the injuries were inflicted by others. This effectively avoids further confrontation with the aggressor, and the victim need not admit to being someone who is willing to tolerate physical abuse. Children, of course, are sometimes unable to report episodes of violence directed against them, and may fear further retaliation if immediate action is not taken to protect them.

The abuser has similar characteristics. Abusive husbands are less assertive with their wives, more likely to have been victims of abuse themselves, and have witnessed parental abuse during their formative years as children.[45] Child abuse and/or incest are likely to occur when the parents stop having sexual relations, the parent of the same sex is absent from the home, the parent of the opposite sex is having a crisis, and the family is abnormal/disorganized.[46] The elderly become vulnerable when living conditions are congested, there are poor cultural mores or changing social behavior, increased financial pressures, and psychiatric or alcohol problems.[47]

Identification of victims of abuse is dependent on the clinician's index of suspicion about potential abuse. Clients may not come forward with the information. Thus, directly asking about how disagreements are resolved, and if this process ever includes physical abuse, may bring the information out.

The second issue for clinicians is to provide safety for the victim. Shelters for battered women are immensely helpful in providing a haven, often in the company of other battered women who can help them define alternatives for themselves. Children can be placed in temporary care situations or admitted to the hospital for observation when abuse is suspected. Protective services for the elderly are a resource for this group. Home visits by community agency members can identify living situations that are unsafe, and alternative sites can be recommended.

Reporting abuse is now mandatory for most health care practitioners and affords them protection from legal suits. The act of reporting is perhaps less of a problem than sensitizing the clinician to problems of abuse and violence and learning how to obtain the necessary information.

To summarize, the dangerous client requires careful screening to avoid overprediction of violence in this group. Nonetheless, clinical judgment should always prevail, rather than second guessing of the court's ultimate decision in confining the client for long-term care. With respect to victims of abuse, the clinician must (1) determine the presence of abuse, (2) evaluate the potential danger in the environment, and (3) facilitate removal of the client from the abusive environment if at all possible.

Clinical Application

The following cases will be used to demonstrate the variability in clinical presentations of clients considered dangerous by the psychiatric emergency staff. In this discussion no follow-up of the cases will be given, since this is typically not known to the clinician until after a decision has been made about the client's potential for violence. Thus, these cases may represent an overprediction of violence, but it is hoped that they will illustrate the problem-solving process of the clinician in determining immediate dangerousness as it applies to planning intervention strategies. The criteria presented in the previous section will be reviewed in an attempt to apply research findings to the clinical examples.

Clinical Example 5-1

The client is a 40-year-old black male brought to the emergency room by the police after he was found verbally harassing customers in the downtown shopping area. He believes that he is a colonel in the army and that those around him should follow his orders. His interactions are intense, loud, and intimidating. He refuses to cooperate with MSE testing and emphatically denies any need for psychiatric treatment. He also denies past psychiatric treatment. He seems very suspicious of the staff's motives but does not manifest or threaten physical violence.

The obvious problem for the clinician is to determine the future dangerousness of this man, since he is unlikely to admit himself voluntarily for treatment. Should he be detained against his will if efforts to convince him to be a voluntary client fail? His behavior has been threatening to the staff, although he has not threatened to harm anyone and did not commit a violent act prior to being brought in by the police. Like the police, the clinician is likely to feel anxious in this man's presence, and without a sufficient number of security personnel on hand would not attempt to ask him to do something he did not want to do. It also seems foolish to provoke this man in order to *prove* that he would be violent under the right circumstances.

Returning to the variables associated with short-term violence, this man meets some, but not all, of the criteria for dangerousness. First, he is paranoid and suspicious. His mannerisms are intense, he is male, and he may have come from a disadvantaged environment or live in one now. Confinement to the hospital may be seen as a provocative event, making him dangerous once admitted. On the other hand, if he is not admitted, any number of environmental events may provoke him, given the intensity of his delusions. Data not immediately available include a previous history of violent acts, a previous psychiatric history, and the etiology of his immediate problem.

In this particular situation, the emergency room staff decided to err on the side of involuntary confinement secondary to the intensity of this man's manner, and the fact that the police were summoned by local shop owners, who had also feared for their safety.

This situation is somewhat analogous to being unable to define which clients are prevented from suicidal behavior by treatment methods. Might this man become more dangerous if left in the community without treatment for his psychotic thinking? Although we may never be able to answer that question, it seems more difficult to allow an intimidating, psychotic individual to return to the community only to injure an innocent bystander. Currently, the decision to admit a client involuntarily rests with the medical and legal establishments. The psychiatric nurse's role must remain focused at the clinical level, where predictions of violence are based on clinical information. Whether or not the civil commitment process would ultimately commit this client is less of an issue than articulating the reasons for labeling this man as potentially dangerous. Although it is important to interpret the legal restrictions of commitment laws, this is only one aspect of the decision to confine a client until the commitment hearing can take place.

The next case illustrates the difficulty in confining clients at the request of family members who have become exhausted in caring for a mentally ill member who remains unwilling to seek psychiatric care.

Clinical Example 5–2

The client is a 24-year-old white single male brought to the emergency service by his elderly parents. He is currently living with his parents, who have become more concerned about his bizarre behavior. This man has a long history of psychiatric admissions and outpatient treatment for chronic paranoid schizophrenia. He stopped taking his medication three weeks ago, and since that time has become more reclusive, alternating with verbally abusive behavior toward his parents. There have not been any physically violent episodes, but the family is concerned about their ability to care for their son in the future. On examination the client is marginally cooperative, answering some of the cognitive questions from the MSE. He denies having hallucinations or delusions but seems preoccupied with his thoughts. He has also been sniffing glue recently.

The short-term predictors in this case indicate that there is some risk of future violence. The client is male, under the age of thirty, diagnosed as paranoid schizophrenic, and might be experiencing more acute symptoms secondary to discontinuing his medication. His recent glue sniffing may also put him at risk for a violent episode secondary to organic mental changes. He has not, however, been physically violent in the past, and his interactions vary fron none to irritable verbal behavior.

This client's family may be at increased risk, since many cases of violence involve family members or close personal acquaintances. The risk to the family may also come in the form of exhaustion from their daily supervision of his behavior and activities. Since he has not threatened them directly or shared any delusional plans to harm them specifically, the *Tarasoff* decision (e.g., the duty to warn intended victims of potential harm) would not be applicable here.

The first approach to this client might be to convince him to seek voluntary hospitalization. He has been in treatment many times before, which might lessen his fear of another hospitalization. Refusal of hospitalization would force the clinician to decide if reinstitution of medication on an outpatient basis might lessen his agitation. In the absence of full cooperation with these plans, the decision to confine this client involuntarily would be very difficult. Here is a clearer example of a client who *might* be dangerous in the future, particularly if and when his psychotic symptoms become more pronounced. At this time, he is not as likely to be dangerous in the near future.

Interventions could be directed toward the family. They might be advised to seek commitment on their own through the court and be prompted to notify the police in the event of more disturbed behavioral changes.

The staff was eventually able to convince this man to admit himself voluntarily to the psychiatric unit in order to reestablish his medication regimen in the hope of becoming more stabilized.

The last case focuses on dangerousness in the elderly, and the overlap between the legal and mental health care systems.

Clinical Example 5–3

The client is a 75-year-old female brought in by the police. They were summoned by a local grocery store owner who had asked them to remove the client from his premises. She had been pitching mayonnaise jars from the shelves of his store at passing motorists. On examination the client was disheveled and looked rather like a typical "bag person." She was relatively uncooperative in answering questions, but was not abusive or assaultive to the emergency room staff. Her thinking was loose and tangential, and there was some evidence of delusional material.

The violent potential of this woman has already been demonstrated by her actions prior to arriving in the emergency room. What motivated her behavior is unclear, although she may be psychotic and potentially demented. Her ability to care for herself is less than optimal, although she does not appear physically ill or likely to be so in the immediate future.

Since this woman has commited a crime, namely, destruction of property, there could be cause for pressing charges against her. The severity of the crime is not such that this would be essential. Her arrival at the emergency room rather than the jail is likely due to the well-established working relationship between the psychiatric emergency staff and the local police department. There are adequate mental health resources in the community to care for such a woman. Thus, putting her in jail would serve little purpose in correcting the situation.

Without an incident of violence, this woman would not have been brought to the psychiatric emergency service. Her mental illness is not severe enough to prevent her from caring for herself, although her standard of living is not what we might call adequate. Since she was not suicidal at the time of the interview, there were no grounds for involuntary confinement on this basis. Her recent assaultive behavior and evidence of a mental disorder are, however, sufficient grounds for the police to sign commitment papers and have her hospitalized.

Summary

Assessment of dangerousness is proving more difficult for the mental health profession than imagined. Criteria have begun to emerge from research studies about those clients most likely to engage in violent behavior over a short period of time. Nonetheless, it will undoubtedly be some time before these criteria for commitment are precisely defined.

In the interim, the clinician must rely on the psychiatric assessment, known risk factors for violence, and the client's life as it may precipitate or discourage violence. Common sense is also useful in prioritizing the data in each clinical situation. If the client has been violent and little has changed to prevent further violence, the risk is probably still high. Thus, regardless of the recent decisions being made in local courts, there is still an obligation to identify, and hold if necessary, those clients at high risk. The decision to commit rests with the legal system, but the decision to screen clients for *potential* risk still remains with the clinician.

Lastly, the care of victims of violence also relies on the data on dangerous behavior. Educating victims about the potential risk in their environment is one method for ensuring their safety. For those clients at risk for harm and unable to secure resources on their own (e.g., children and the elderly), more aggressive interventions may be necessary to protect them and enlist the aid of community agencies on their behalf.

References

1. Scott, P. D.: Assessing dangerousness in criminals. *British Journal of Psychiatry, 131,* 127–142, 1977.
2. Tupin, J.: The violent patient: A strategy for management and diagnosis. *Hospital and Community Psychiatry, 34,* 37–40, 1983.
3. Monahan, J.: *The Clinical Prediction of Violent Behavior: Crime and Delinquency Issues.* Rockville, Md.: National Institute of Mental Health, 1981.
4. Ibid.
5. Ennis, B., and Emery, R.: *The Rights of Mental Patients.* New York: Avon Books, 1978.
6. Pfohl, S. J.: From whom will we be protected? Comparative ap-

proaches to the assessment of dangerousness. *International Journal of Law and Psychiatry, 2,* 55–78, 1979.

7. Hays, J. R.: Ethics of prediction of future dangerousness. *Psychological Reports, 49,* 593–594, 1981.

8. Shah, S.: Dangerousness and civil commitment of the mentally ill: Some public policy considerations. *American Journal of Psychiatry, 132,* 501–505, 1975.

9. Fottrell, E.: Violent behavior by psychiatric patients. *British Journal of Hospital Medicine, 25,* 28–38, 1981.

10. Scott, op. cit.

11. Rofman, E. S.; Askinazi, C.; and Fant, E.: The prediction of dangerous behavior in emergency civil commitment. *American Journal of Psychiatry, 137,* 1061–1064, 1980.

12. Greenland, C.: The prediction and management of dangerous behavior: Social policy issues. *International Journal of Law and Psychiatry, 1,* 205–222, 1978.

13. Monahan, J.: The prediction of violent behavior: Toward a second generation of theory and policy. *American Journal of Psychiatry, 141,* 10–15. 1984.

14. Pfohl, op. cit.

15. Shah, op. cit.

16. Rofman et al., op. cit.

17. Dubin, W. R.: Evaluating and managing the violent patient. *Annals of Emergency Medicine, 10,* 481–485, 1981.

18. Kroll, J., and Mackenzie, T.: When psychiatrists are liable: Risk management and violent patients. *Hospital and Community Psychiatry, 34,* 29–36, 1983.

19. Rofman et al., op. cit.

20. Monahan (1981), op. cit.

21. Geis, G.: The framework of violence. *Topics in Emergency Medicine, 3,* 1–7, 1982.

22. Tupin, op. cit.

23. Ibid.

24. Monahan (1981), op. cit.

25. Ibid.

26. Tupin, op. cit.

27. Ibid.

28. Coutant, N. S.: Rage: Implied neurological correlates. *Journal of Neurosurgical Nursing, 14,* 28–33, 1982.

29. Tupin, op. cit.

30. Ibid.

31. Tupin, J. P.; Mahar, D.; and Smith, D.: Two types of violent offenders with psychosocial descriptors. *Diseases of the Nervous System, 34,* 356–363, 1973.
32. Prins, H. A.: Dangerous people or dangerous situations? Some implications for assessment and management. *Medical Science Law, 21,* 125–133, 1981.
33. Rada, R.: The violent patient: Rapid assessment and management. *Psychosomatics, 22,* 101–109, 1981.
34. Geis, op. cit.
35. Schwartz, D.: Some problems in predicting dangerousness. *Psychiatric Quarterly, 52,* 79–83, 1980.
36. Slaby, A. E.: Emergency psychiatry: An update. *Hospital and Community Psychiatry, 32,* 687–698, 1981.
37. Shipley, S. B., and Sylvester, D. C.: Professional's attitudes toward violence in close relationships. *Journal of Emergency Nursing, 8,* 88–91, 1982.
38. Goodstein, R. K., and Page, A. W.: Battered wife syndrome: Overview of dynamics and treatment. *American Journal of Psychiatry, 138,* 1036–1043, 1981.
39. Kirkland, K.: Assessment and treatment of family violence. *The Journal of Family Practice, 14,* 713–718, 1982.
40. Rosenbaum, A., and O'Leary, K.: Marital violence: Characteristics of abusive couples. *Journal of Consulting and Clinical Psychology, 49,* 63–71, 1981.
41. Gayford, J. J.: Battered wives. *Medicine, Science, and the Law, 15,* 237–245, 1975.
42. Husain, A., and Chapel, J.: History of incest in girls admitted to a psychiatric hospital. *American Journal of Psychiatry, 140,* 591–593, 1983.
43. Tokarski, P.: Sexual abuse of the child. *Topics in Emergency Medicine, 3,* 15–21, 1982.
44. Falcioni, D.: Assessing the abused elderly. *Journal of Gerontological Nursing, 8,* 208–212, 1982.
45. Kirkland, op. cit.
46. Lieske, A. M.: Incest: An overview. *Perspectives in Psychiatric Care, 19,* 59–63, 1981.
47. Falcioni, op. cit.

CHAPTER 6

INTERNAL ENABLING FACTORS

The following three chapters will examine the variables associated with discharge planning in the psychiatric emergency service. Determining the most appropriate discharge plan for the client is an *interactional process*. The *clinician* is responsible for evaluating the clinical problems and suggesting the most efficacious form of care. The *client* is responsible for deciding if the treatment options are reasonable and then following through with the recommendations.

Compliance or *adherence* (these two terms essentially identify the same process) commonly refers to the amount of cooperation by the client in following the treatment recommendations of the health care provider. The degree of anticipated compliance by the client will markedly alter the disposition plan in most cases. For example, the client with a personality disorder who is moderately suicidal may receive outpatient care if the plan is agreeable to the *client* and if there are family members available to offer support until treatment is underway. If the client is not receptive to outpatient care and has few supportive individuals available, inpatient care may be necessary to provide a safe, protective environment.

The extent to which an individual values the care plan is dependent on multiple variables. These variables have been indentified and researched within medical sociology and have become known collectively as the Health Belief Model.[1] These studies attempt to understand the motivations and constraints involved in the utilization of health care services by individuals. Terms used to describe aspects of health care utilization include: *predisposing factors* (e.g., individual and family characteristics which exist prior to the onset of illness and result in differences in the propensity to use health services); *enabling factors* (e.g., family and community resources which allow access to health care); and *need* (e.g., the perceived degree of illness requiring care).[2]

This chapter and Chapter 7 will address the enabling factors (internal and external, respectively) affecting a client's decision to engage in health care. We are not using *enabling factors* in its strictest sense, but rather as a generic term that describes the likelihood of a client's compliance with treatment recommendations. Compliance/adherence will be discussed in Chapter 8 as an interactional concept between the client and the clinician in negotiating follow-up care.[3]

Clinical Content

Overview

The Health Belief Model is an organizational concept that includes all relevant forces known to influence a client's decision to seek care. Becker and Maiman have recently reviewed the existing models of health utilization and presented a comprehensive model containing the cumulative variables in a multidimensional framework.[4] Based on their revised Health Belief Model, we will review those factors most closely associated with internal enabling factors.

Internal enabling factors refer to the intrapsychic values and experiences which dictate the use of health care services under certain conditions. These internal variables are organized into three major groups:

    I. Health threat variables
   II. Knowledge variables
  III. Health care evaluation variables

Each of these groups will be reviewed separately, along with the items which comprise them.

Before discussing these three groups, it is important to understand the stages of illness which serve as motivational stimuli for the client.[5] The preillness stage refers to *health-seeking behavior* (i.e., those activities undertaken by the client to prevent illness and maintain health). Once symptoms appear, the next stage is *illness-seeking behavior* (i.e., those activities aimed at obtaining a diagnosis and treatment for symptoms). The third stage is *sick-role behavior* (i.e., those activities which remove symptoms or prevent further complications from an established illness). The health-related behaviors of each category vary among individuals and different cultural groups.

Table 6-1 lists the intrapersonal variables known to affect the client's propensity toward any or all of these help-seeking behaviors.[6] These factors are grouped into those most influenced by experiential/developmental events and those which are specific to the illness episode. Experiential/developmental factors include trust, previous experiences of oneself and others with the health care system, knowledge of symptoms and health care treatments, value of the health care system in general, and the availability and value accorded a "lay evaluation system" (advice from family and friends about the need for care and the seriousness of the symptoms). These items represent accumulated lifetime experiences and the cultural values of the family or community.

The factors specific to each illness episode have a more direct influence on the client, particularly if the symptoms are severe, frequent, and disrupt valued social/occupational roles. Psychiatric care also raises issues of attribution and stigma. If the individual believes that the psychiatric symptoms are the result of a physical problem or fears becoming identified as a psychiatric client, there will be fewer opportunities to engage the client in treatment. The factors in Table

TABLE 6-1   Intrapersonal Factors Affecting Help-Seeking Behavior

Experiential/developmental factors
  Trust
  Previous experience of oneself and others with health care
  Knowledge of illness and health care
  Value of health care
  Reliance on the lay evaluation system
Episode-specific
  Attribution
  Stigma
  Insight
  Hopefulness versus helplessness
  Degree of threat
  Seriousness of the symptoms
  Disruption of the life-style

6-1 are affected by specific illness episodes and by each contact with the health care system. Thus, the psychiatric emergency visit, although brief, is an opportunity to align the client positively with psychiatric care providers.

Many of the concepts inherent in help-seeking behavior are commonly understood by the client. They are not, however, always uppermost in the clinician's mind, since we too often assume that individuals who appear seeking care are willing to follow the advice we dispense, without regard for the internal and external resources of each individual.

Understanding the motivating and constraining forces in health care utilization is becoming increasingly important given current trends toward self-care and consumerism. The clinician should remember that the ultimate responsbility for carrying out medical regimens rests with the client, and that the clinician's responsibility is to facilitate the client's recovery in those settings appropriate for and acceptable to the client.

Health Threat Variables

This concept refers to the amount of threat necessary to motivate clients to seek care during times of physical illness.[7,8] The circumstances necessary for clients to seek care include the seriousness of the symptoms, the perceived susceptibility of the client, and the disruption in well-being and social role performance secondary to the symptoms.[9] Individuals are more likely to seek health care if symptoms are severe, frequent, and disabling.

The seriousness of the health threat is mitigated by avoiding the sick role and by labeling the consequences of the illness as minimal. If fear and anxiety are low, the client may also delay seeking health care. Conversely, if fear and anxiety reach panic proportions, the client may become immobilized and unable to seek care voluntarily.

When the threat of illness is a physical one, the client is usually the initiator of help-seeking behavior. When emotional problems dominate the clinical picture, others may define the illness and become the primary motivators in arranging for health care services. The process of evaluating the health threat is the same for client-initiated and other-initiated help-seeking behavior. In other words, assessing the magnitude of the health threat is the same for others witnessing the symptoms as it is for the client experiencing them.

A health threat is particularly difficult to estimate in the psychiatric population, where insight, judgment, and motivation are affected by the illness itself. Psychotic symptoms, organic mental changes, and serious personality disorders are frequently not recognized by the client, or the symptoms may seem egosyntonic with existing reality distortions. Clients may also attribute their dysfunctional emotional states to current stressors, life events, and impending life changes. Thus, the client may not view the psychiatric system as the most appropriate setting for the amelioration of discomfort. Instead, clients may externalize the cause of their discomfort, hoping that environmental changes will produce the needed relief.

Acceptance of the sick role is, therefore, necessary to ensure cooperation with psychiatric care plans. This is dependent on the client's level of denial and tolerance of psychiatric symptoms. Pressure may need to be exerted by the family/social system in order to convince the client of the need for care. This is a critical step in magnifying the health threat to a level where cooperation is forthcoming.

Evaluation of a health threat is measured by the history of the current problem and the route taken by the client in arriving for care. Problems that have existed for a long time indicate a tolerance for symptoms and the likelihood that others have defined the problem on the client's behalf. On a more positive note, long-standing problems may serve to motivate those individuals who have exhausted alternative health care methods and are thus ready to utilize the formal psychiatric care system.

The *types* of alternative treatment methods employed will alert the clinician to the value accorded the lay evaluation system and the kinds of supports available to the client. Religious and folk medicine resources may need to be included in designing a care plan that is acceptable to the client and his or her social/lay support system.

Knowledge Variables

In order for clients to approach the health care system, they must posess some knowledge that allows them to recognize symptoms and identify the problem as a danger to existing health. This knowledge is a composite of general knowledge and disease/medical familiarity. Fabrega's model of *illness-behavior,* presented in Table 6–2, lists the steps involved in illness recognition and help-seeking behavior.[10] Steps I, II, and III pertain to knowledge variables, whereas step IV refers to health care evaluation.

Knowledge variables are closely tied to health threat variables. Without a system for judging the seriousness of the problem and the

TABLE 6–2   Illness-Seeking Behavior

Step I: Illness recognition with labeling
    Internal clues: health threat
    External clues: lay evaluation
Step II: "Illness disvalue"
    Disability
    Discomfort
    Stigma
    Social/psychological disruption
Step III: Treatment plans
    Self-care
    Lay versus Formal medical care
Step IV: Evaluation of treatment plans
    Probability of reducing "illness disvalue"
    Treatment benefit
    Cost/benefit ratio

Adapted from Fabrega, H.: Toward a model of illness behavior. *Medical Care, 11,* 470–484, 1973.

resource most likely to be helpful, the client and/or family are unable to initiate traditional health care behavior. Clients experiencing their first episode of emotional problems may have no reference point for attributing the changes to a mental illness episode. Future episodes of psychiatric dysfunction may be recognized sooner, with delays in seeking care related to previous negative experiences with the health care system.

Evaluation of the client's knowledge of the illness provides the clinician with opportunities to educate and socialize the client about future treatment. It is useful to help the client recognize the internal and external evidence of impending problems. Similarly, the degree of threat, danger, and disability may facilitate client acceptance of treatment recommendations.

Socializing or preparing the client for further treatment is also likely to affect compliance. Entering treatment settings for the first time can be threatening and can elicit fantasies that prevent cooperation. The client can be reassured about the setting and accurately informed about what to expect in the way of treatment. Here it is important to share knowledge, while simultaneously identifying the client's rights and responsibilities as a consumer of health care.

Evaluation of Health Care Variables

These variables include many of the internal values held by the client with respect to the health care system in general. Prior to seeking care in a particular setting, the client will judge the value of the service, his or her skepticism about health care in general, the cost/benefit ratio, and personal goals in maintaining health.[11]

Clients will value health care based on their own previous experiences, the reputation of the resource as judged by themselves and the community, and the perceived quality of care they are likely to receive. This is important to consider with psychiatric clients who have been treated previously in settings where the care was not valued. In the process of making a referral, the clinician must evaluate the client's preference for treatment in a particular setting. Clients with positive experiences may resist referral to a new setting where they are unfamiliar with staff and treatment practices, preferring to return to a setting that is familiar. Similarly, others may resist returning to a treatment setting associated with poor previous care.

The cost/benefit ratio must be evaluated for clients. This includes the emotional benefits as well as the monetary and emotional costs. Skepticism of and low benefit from health care will negatively affect compliance.

Assessment Process

The value of the Health Belief Model is directly related to the reliability of the data collected. Thus, the clinician must remain cognizant of the inherent authority in the health care provider's role, which often precludes clients' disclosure of information considered unacceptable. In order to elicit the most reliable data from the client, the clinician must provide a safe atmosphere wherein the discussion of personal agendas for care and impediments to follow-up can be discussed.

The discussion of internal enabling factors alone deserves an assessment process. The data listed in this section provide a framework for determining the health values of the client. This gives the clinician important clues to the client's degree of concern about the immediate problem and the kinds of treatment valued by the client in restoring the mental health status. Additionally, the client's social system has its own beliefs about treatment which may simultaneously influence the client's decision to seek care.

Since many of the psychiatric conditions seen in the emergency service are likely to be chronic, health beliefs are useful markers for predicting future compliance. The values held by clients can be modified by the experiences of a single visit. Thus, the clinician is responsible for sensitively addressing the client's preconceived ideas about care and the course of action valued by the client and his or her support system.

Clinical Application

Unfortunately, health belief information is not routinely sought in clinical evaluations. This omission is undoubtedly related to the clinical belief that there are only limited options for health care and the fear that clients may request care that is not available or hold beliefs about care that cannot be integrated into existing treatment modalities. Regardless of the magnitude of the idiosyncracies in the client's belief system, these data are important predictors of future utilization patterns. Without a thorough understanding of the client's values, the negotiation for care may become a power struggle or abort the usefulness of a disposition plan.

Case material will now be presented which documents the particular values of the client in question.

Clinical Example 6–1

The client is a 75-year-old white, widowed female who came to the emergency room for treatment of "red spots" on her hands. During the triage process, the emergency room nurse noted that the client thought that the spots were caused by the laser beams her neighbors had been shooting at her. She was promptly referred to psychiatry. On examination the client was well dressed, clean, and appeared to be in good health. She repeated her story about the laser beams. She denied having had previous psychiatric care and stated that we probably thought she was crazy. In spite of her good appearance, this woman had been sleeping under her dining room table, with a rubber sheet over her to prevent the "rays" from doing further harm.

In this case, the problem that prompted the client's illness-seeking behavior was not the major concern for the medical staff. The staff found her story so bizarre that she was immediately referred to psychiatry before her hands were evaluated. The client was aware of the effect of her story on health care providers, which perhaps indicated previous experience with psychiatric treatment settings. Her inability to separate reality from psychotic thinking was also a factor in her unwillingness to seek psychiatric care.

This client's physical health threat variables (red spots) enabled her to seek medical care, but the psychiatric problem (fear of laser beams) was not severe enough to motivate her to seek psychiatric care. Since the psychotic thoughts had become integrated into her life-style, she had more tolerance for these symptoms and little need to enter the sick role.

The fear of her neighbors associated with the psychiatric symptoms led the client to seek help from her landlord, rather than using the psychiatric system to help alleviate her delusions. We later learned that she had been in psychiatric treatment before. She had failed to learn the meaning of her symptoms or the potential value of psychiatric care. As we attempted to convince this woman to seek voluntary admission to the psychiatric unit, she shared her concern about being placed in a nursing home if she were admitted to the hospital. This had previously frightened her on another admission and caused her to move out of town upon discharge from the hospital. After some discussion, she was finally convinced to admit herself to the inpatient psychiatric unit.

We focused on her need to get relief from the home situation and the potential benefit of psychiatric treatment. We also stressed her options as a voluntary client and her right to be discharged when she felt ready. The graduate nursing student who had worked with her in the emergency service agreed to see her during her hospitalization in an effort to build trust and reassure her that she need not go to a nursing home unless she wished. The positive outcome in this situation (admission to the unit) was directly related to an understanding of the health care evaluation variables which were meaningful to this client. Her fear of a nursing home placement was strong enough to override psychiatric health threat variables and knowledge of the illness. Convincing her of the magnitude of her emotional problem was also useless at this juncture and might have discouraged her from trusting us further.

The next case illustrates the effect of dependency on health care evaluation variables and a low tolerance for health threat symptoms.

Clinical Example 6–2

The client is a 37-year-old white divorced female who presents to the emergency service in an agitated, distraught state. She is threatening suicide, evasive in describing the immediate crisis, and uncooperative in sharing information about herself. She is well known to the emergency room staff, having made several previous visits and attempted suicide on other occasions. Her existing diagnosis is borderline personality disorder, and she has had several repeated admissions to the state hospital and the local inpatient psychiatric service. She is currently requesting admission to the psychiatric unit.

This situation is common in the psychiatric emergency service once clients are socialized into using the emergency room as an entry to the hospital setting. This client has obviously had numerous experiences with the psychiatric care system and approaches it for care during critical times. What is also evident is the limited repertoire that she displays when seeking help. She is unable to solve the immediate crisis, preferring instead to be admitted to the hospital.

Clients with an inability to discuss their problems during a crisis are extremely difficult to treat during an emergency visit. They tend to defy interventions aimed at reducing the anxiety associated with the immediate symptoms, and seek relief (in the form of admission to the hospital) from their problems.

Using the health belief indexes associated with internal enabling factors, this client would score high on health threat, knowledge of resources and symptoms, and positive attitude toward inpatient psychiatric treatment settings. This constellation of variables simultaneously limits the treatment options secondary to the client's intense desire for a *single* option, namely, admission.

The threat of psychiatric symptoms is exaggerated in this client, since she is unable to tolerate the feelings of anxiety and depression which surface during a crisis. The length of her psychiatric and treatment histories may indicate that she has come to value the experience of inpatient psychiatric care, particularly during critical times. The costs of treatment are outweighed by the perceived benefits.

The evaluation of the health threat and health care variables indicates that this woman is unlikely to value alternative modes of therapy at this juncture. When her attitudes are combined with the clinician's assesment of her suicide risk, there may be few options for care outside the hospital setting.

Unfortunately, clients like this woman often frustrate treatment personnel, who feel manipulated by the threat of suicide and restrained from suggesting other treatment options. When inpatient beds are not available, the process of negotiating with clients for outpatient care can be delicate. Since many clients understand the limitations of health care resources, this is a more useful approach than denying their request on the basis of past history and poor compliance with outpatient care.

Outreach care or holding beds may provide an alternative resource that meets safety needs of this client and yet offers a more restrictive environment for care. Clients who have little tolerance for their health threat symptoms and have become attached to the care system require creative treatment plans when their first choice is not available.

The last case describes the influence of the lay evaluation system and the fear of health care treatment.

Clinical Example 6–3

The police arrived at the emergency service with an 80-year-old woman and her 82-year-old sister. The younger sister was brought in by the police, who were called by neighbors. The neighbors became concerned at the client's abuse of her sister when she was found in the yard with a knife. The two women were impeccably dressed, clean, and relatively cooperative during the psychiatric interview. These women have lived together for over 40 years in the family home and have managed their affairs independently. There are no other living relatives. The older sister noted that her sister had become more irritable, forgetful, and paranoid over the past two years. She suspected that her sister was becoming "senile" but resisted psychiatric care for fear of having to place her sister in a nursing home.

This case illustrates the influence that family members or lay evaluation systems can have on help-seeking behavior. The sister who has become paranoid and probably demented is "protected" from health care because the fear of health costs (e.g., nursing home placement) is so great.

The client's lack of insight and independence prevents her from seeking care on her own; thus, the well sister tolerates the health threat variables. In this case, both sisters have tolerated symptoms of paranoid behavior and physical abuse in order to maintain the homeostasis of the family environment.

The perceived lack of benefit to be gained from psychiatric care, coupled with the disruption of daily routines, precluded earlier health care treatment. The threat of a nursing home placement and the older sister's wish to remain with her sister also kept her away from health care settings.

At the time of this visit, the younger sister was involuntarily admitted to the state hospital for care. A subsequent visit occurred about a year later, after both sisters were found with slashed wrists at a local nursing home. As the older sister feared, they were eventually placed in a nursing home together, and were unable to tolerate the environment.

Summary

Internal enabling factors serve as powerful motivators or deterrents to help-seeking behavior. The threat of health care symptoms in conjunction with the assumed seriousness of the illness will motivate clients, or others on their behalf, to approach the health care system.

Previous experience with symptoms provides a historical context for judging subsequent symptoms and the need for formal medical care versus home remedies. Chronic illness gives the client a longer history by which to evaluate the seriousness of symptoms and the costs and benefits of the formal health care system.

Evaluation of health care services similarly modifies the client's preference for care. Poor treatment experiences discourage subsequent use of such services for the same problem, whereas positive experiences reinforce the client's preferences. In psychiatric settings, clinicians often note the preference for inpatient versus outpatient care, or vice versa.

Assessment of clients' internal health belief systems narrows the options and choices for disposition planning to those most valued and likely to be followed. This process also gives the clinician clues about fears, past experiences, and preferences that can be addressed in the emergency service. Without fully understanding the client's beliefs and fears, the process of negotiating treatment plans occurs in a vacuum.

References

1. Maiman, L., and Becker, M. H.: The health belief model: Origins and correlates in psychological theory. *Health Education Monographs, 2,* 336–353, 1974.
2. Anderson, R.: *A Behavioral Model of Families' Use of Health Services.* Chicago: Center for Health Administration Studies, University of Chicago, 1968.

3. Lazare, A.; Eisenthal, S.; and Frank, A.: A negotiated approach to the clinic encounter II: Conflict and negotiation. In: Lazare, A. (ed.), *Outpatient Psychiatry,* Baltimore: Williams & Wilkins, pp. 157–171, 1979.

4. Becker, M. and Maiman, L.: Models of health-related behavior. In: Mechanic, D. (ed.), *Handbook of Health, Health Care, and the Health Professional.* New York: Free Press, pp 539–568, 1983.

5. Kasl, S., and Cobb, S.: Health behavior, illness behavior, sick role behavior. I: Health and illness behavior. II: Sick role behavior. *Archives of Environmental Health, 12,* 246–266, 531–541, 1966.

6. Mechanic, D.: The concept of illness behavior. *Journal of Chronic Diseases, 15,* 189–194, 1962.

7. Rosenstock, I.: The health belief model and prevention health behavior. *Health Education Monographs, 2,* 354–386, 1974.

8. Kasl and Cobb, op. cit.

9. Becker and Maiman, op. cit.

10. Fabrega, H.: Toward a model of illness behavior. *Medical Care, 11,* 470–484, 1973.

11. Becker and Maiman, op. cit.

CHAPTER 7

EXTERNAL ENABLING FACTORS

This chapter will focus on external enabling factors which complement the internal factors reviewed in the previous chapter. According to Becker and Maiman's Health Belief Model, there are three groups of external enabling factors:[1]

Social network variables
Access to health care variables
Demographic variables

As the term *external* indicates, these variables exist independently in the client's environment and exert their influence in interaction with the client's intrapsychic structure. The importance of each variable in disposition planning will vary according to the restrictiveness or resourcefulness that each provides. In other words, an item may *facilitate* the client's entry into a treatment system (e.g., encouragement from the family), or it may *prevent* the client from gaining access to a system (e.g., lack of insurance coverage to pay for services).

Social network variables exert their influence through the support and validation of health care practices by members of the client's support network. *Access variables* determine the type and amount of resources available to the client and the emotional/physical energy required to utilize them. *Demographic variables* include the age, gender, socioeconomic status, education, marital status, and religious preference of the client. These exert an indirect effect on utilization of services through experience, socialization, and economic resources, and are difficult to integrate directly into the treatment plan.

By attending to external variables in the psychiatric emergency service, the clinician attempts to expand the disposition alternatives for clients. Often the resources available from the emergency service are minimal secondary to limited mental health and financial resources for the chronically mentally ill.

The responsibility for finding suitable treatment settings must reside with the *clinician*. Familiarity with community resources, eligibility requirements, and accessibility to care keeps the clinician informed about treatment options. This knowledge provides a range of resources that can be called upon for selected clients. External enabling factors guide the assessment process and offer some measure of the potential for creative interventions.

Clinical Content

Overview

Modifying external enabling conditions requires different approaches in the psychiatric emergency service. These factors, such as access, are often restricted by location, cost of services, waiting lists, and policies which limit the range of services. Demographic variables obviously cannot be changed by the clinician (or the client), but they provide a pattern of service utilization by which the clinician can predict future behavior. Interventions must therefore be directed at persons or settings that are able to facilitate linkage of the client with the setting for continued care. Friends and family members may need to become part of the negotiation for treatment, and the clinician must provide admission information to hospitals and coerce outpatient clinics to make an appointment within a brief period of time.

In this section, we will review the external factors which affect disposition planning and selection of treatment resources. The most obvious treatment setting is not always the one in which the client would prefer to receive care. Thus, the clinician is reminded that negotiation invites the client to disclose treatment preferences and thus adds to the kinds of options likely to be helpful in problem solving. With both client and clinician working on disposition plans, alternatives expand and compliance may be increased.

Social Network Variables

The composite model of Becker and Maiman lists the following social network variables:

> Nonkin interaction
> Communication inside and outside the network
> Participation
> Social pressures and forces
> Traditional and ethnic values
> Communication with spouse or others
> Friendship network
> Conjugal communication structure[2]

These items encompass the variables known to exert their influence through the individual's social system. Members of ethnic groups, married persons, and those with extensive social resources have numerous networks which may influence treatment decisions. As this list indicates, most of the influence from the social network comes in the form of communication resources/patterns that are available to the client and can be used by the clinician to determine the best plan for alleviating the immediate problem. These resources do not necessarily predict that the client will accept the treatment recommendations of the clinician (e.g., supportive individuals may not agree with the treatment recommendations or will not force the client to seek care involuntarily).

The clinician must understand the relationships that exist in the client's network and the influence that each member contributes to health care decisions. If the network is to facilitate the clinician's goals for care, the most influential individuals must become aligned with the treatment team and enlist the cooperation of the client. Thus, part of the assessment of the support networks must focus on the interactional patterns, any "hidden agendas" of the client or family members, and the key people likely to enlist the client's cooperation and act in his or her best interests. Hidden agendas refer to unspoken concerns or plans which network members hope will be solved if their advice is followed.

When a less extensive social network exists, the clinician may become very influential in directing the client toward treatment resources. In this instance, it is also important to understand the reasons for a limited social network, such as loss of the network through death, divorce, or relocation, or the client's inability to tolerate close relationships, which might preclude an easy transition into a treatment setting for care.

The social network of a client includes:

Individuals with whom the client has contact for goods and services

The relationships *with* those individuals

The relationships *among* those individuals within the social network[3,4]

The type of support available from the members of the network will vary from individual to individual. As a general rule, networks provide support in four basic ways:[5]

Emotional: affective concern, caring, empathy

Appraisal: evaluation of data and comparison of issues

Instrumental: direct aid—time, energy, monetary support

Informational: advice, suggestions, directions

These types of support may be available in differing degrees and may not exist in the amount or form required to assist the clinician and client during the psychiatric emergency. For example, the client's family may have financial resources to assist with hospitalization, but in the absence of settings for inpatient care it is more useful to spend time with the client until hospitalization can be arranged. Thus, the essential factor becomes the *needed* rather than the *available* type of support.[6]

Another qualifier of support networks is their *structural* and *relational properties.*[7] These terms refer to the quantity and quality of the client's network, respectively. Structural properties measure the size and density (e.g., interconnectedness) of the supportive network available to the client. Relational properties include content, intensity, and reciprocity. *Content* describes the contact links that bring the client and the network together. More precisely, it refers to the context of the relationship (e.g., work, hobbies, religious organizations). *Intensity* measures the closeness of the relationships, whereas *reciprocity* refers to the give-and-take between the individual and the network.

The relational properties of the network provide some predictive measure of the social support system's ability to facilitate compliance with treatment recommendations. The actual number of members in the network is less important than the types of relationships which exist and can be called upon during a crisis. Members influence internal enabling factors through lay evaluation of health threats (the severity of symptoms and need for care) and evaluation of services (the best setting for care). External enabling conditions are positively influenced by a lay evaluation which values the service and the need for care. Network members can also be instrumental in reducing access barriers by taking the client to appointments, providing monetary support for services, and so on.

The support network may also serve as a treatment resource during periods of care provision. Care activities may include protection of the client from harm, reminders to take medication, transportation to clinic appointments, and supportive listening.

The duration and intensity of the support network provide an index of the availability and interest of members in caring for the client during the psychiatric emergency. Some networks will have depleted their resources during a lengthy preadmission phase; others will have become exhausted after months or years of caring for a chronically ill member and refuse further treatment burdens, looking to the system for respite care.

Demographic Variables

Demographic variables are useful predictors of help-seeking behavior in *groups* of individuals, and therefore have only limited clinical application. They are, however, good indicators of who uses particular services under differing circumstances. For the psychiatric emergency service, demographic studies have noted that lower socioeconomic groups, women, divorced, widowed, or single individuals, and clients aged 20 to 39 are most highly represented.[8] These individuals are considered the high-risk populations for whom special services could be planned.

For the lower socioeconomic groups this is important, since resources are limited primarily by financial constraints. The clinician needs to know the availability of community resources for the indigent and the eligibility requirements of local hospitals that may admit clients without third-party coverage. Community mental health resources are often planned according to diagnostic and catchment criteria, thus further complicating the referral mechanisms for clients.

This kind of community information is frequently cited as most important for the psychiatric emergency clinician in finding suitable secondary treatment resources for clients.[9] It is this combination of demographic and access variables that requires the most creative use of services by the psychiatric emergency clinician. Considerable energy is needed to learn the requirements of hospitals for admitting clients or the amount of outpatient care provided by welfare agencies.

Demographic variables also exert their influence through the experiences and the socialization process that are part of the client's background. Whether or not clients are aligned with the folk medicine system or the traditional medical system will determine their affiliation for subsequent care. Ethnic and cultural experiences will determine how willing the client may be to try a new health care setting versus returning to one that is valued and known to the family and is therefore more acceptable.

Access to Health Care Variables

This set of variables includes specific items that hinder or help the client in approaching a particular health care setting. The composite model of Becker and Maiman lists the following *access variables:*

Constraints
Psychological costs
Ability to pay
Availability
Physician choice
Access
Resources available in the setting[10]

Many of these factors are commonly known issues that affect the client's willingness and eligibility to seek care in specified settings, yet they may be overlooked during the evaluation process. The emphasis on monetary constraints is well known in mental health care, where public financing has traditionally given the indigent client access to psychiatric services. Long-standing mental health problems are typically associated with decreased earning power and restricted third-party coverage for health care. Thus, most chronically ill clients are forced to use public mental health facilities, which easily become saturated.

As noted in Chapter 1, the emergency service has few access barriers to care, and thus is an attractive resource for several reasons.

One is that clients need not wait for an appointment, and can therefore seek care at the time of greatest need and motivation. Second, financial barriers are lessened since emergency services rarely turn clients away. Third, waiting times are decreased, reducing the frustration associated with delays. Fourth, the emergency service is an entry point to the hospital, and clients requesting admission need only make one stop. Fifth, the service is known to have medical, nursing, and social work staff available, thus providing a multiplicity of services in one setting.

The characteristics listed above are ideal in reducing access barriers. Obviously, services designed for emergency purposes are expensive to operate and cannot possibly deliver long-term care to clients under these circumstances. Attempts to refer clients to secondary treatment settings must therefore *match* the client's preferences and resources with the setting's limitations and services.

Selection of a suitable treatment resource depends on the clinical problem and the type of care needed. This ensures that the client will receive the most appropriate care and will have access to clinicians knowledgeable in treating the immediate problem. For example, clients who require medication or an evaluation for medication must be referred to settings with access to psychiatrists. Similarly, the agency must be proficient in treating the types of problems the client is experiencing; otherwise the referral is likely to be rejected by the secondary agency.

The financial resources of the client will also determine the setting where the client is eligible to receive care. If insurance is not adequate to cover the expense of care, publicly financed agencies will be enlisted. These agencies are often catchmented (i.e., eligibility is determined by income level and address), necessitating correct demographic and financial information about the client before attempting a referral.

Beyond these obvious limitations on access, the remaining factors are a matter of client preference. Factors such as the client's willingness to use a particular facility or the ability to travel to the clinic are important. Clients who are employed may have limited time for appointments; others will have child care responsibilities that might interfere with keeping an appointment. The stigma of the setting for each client is also important to understand. Mental health facilities are often prominent in the community and their reputations precede them. The same may be true of Veterans' Hospitals. The client's perception of the setting will disclose much about the likelihood of compliance with the treatment plan.

At this point in the negotiation for care, it is extremely useful to ask the client what he or she has in mind. This can be most illuminating and may often simplify the grander schemes designed by the clinician. Clients may have a particular clinic in mind, or may feel satisfied with the emergency service and require no further care.

For those clients with serious problems, the clinician may need to ensure a closer fit between client and setting for follow-up care. The decision about inpatient versus outpatient care is the first step in the decision-making process. The use of the client's support network may enable the more disturbed client to remain an outpatient if the family is willing to ensure compliance with outpatient treatment. In the absence of this type of resource, the client may need to be admitted to a hospital until the immediate crisis is better controlled. Again, the choice of setting will depend on eligibility and availability of resources (i.e., of both the client and the treatment setting).

The emergency service's clinician has many opportunities to influence access barriers in the community.[11] Knowledge of the eligibility requirements of clinics and hospitals will expedite transfers to other settings for continued care. The referral process can be shortened when the clinician is known to the referring agency and an atmosphere of trust is established between the two. This often lessens the burden on the client or the family by eliminating another evaluation procedure in order to begin the process of treatment. By understanding the admission procedures of other hospitals and clinics, the clinician becomes sensitive to the barriers likely to be faced by the client.

This up-to-date information about community resources will prevent obvious treatment failures from occurring. If a clinic has a long waiting list or is not accepting clients, the use of that resource in an emergency seems unwarranted. Merely directing the client toward a resource indicates some expectation that motivation is high. This is rarely the case, however, since clients seek care during critical times, and lack sufficient energy and ego strength to wait until the health care system has time for them.

Attempting to obtain an appointment for a client from an understaffed, overwhelmed clinic can be an eye-opening experience. One is often told that the client will have to come over, give some demographic information, and then wait until an appointment is mailed. Once seen in the clinic by an admitting officer, the client may wait an undetermined amount of time before being assigned to a therapist for care. These types of treatment restrictions can deter even highly motivated clients.

Assessment of External Enabling Factors

Determining the enabling factors for each client requires a review of the social support network, the access barriers, and the interaction of these assets and liabilities with the interpersonal style of the client. The social network is only as helpful as the client allows it to be. If the relationships are strained, or the client is too ill to respond to the support and/or limits imposed by the members, their effectiveness is curtailed.

For those clients with limited social networks, the clinician may need to determine the availability of previously untapped resources such as neighbors, a landlady, or a new friend who could be called upon to provide some measure of care during the immediate crisis. These individuals might be called upon to transport the client to a hospital or clinic for care, or watch the client overnight until a regularly scheduled appointment can be kept. In these instances, both the client's capacity and the social network's require assessment. Again, is the client willing and psychologically able to follow the instructions of others and seek care at a predetermined site?

Summary

External enabling factors determine the type of setting where the client is willing, eligible, and able to receive follow-up care. The limitations imposed by external factors come from financial constraints, limited social network resources, and preexisting experiences which decrease the client's willingness to seek additional care. Agreement between the client and the clinician about future health care needs will improve the client's likelihood of compliance with treatment recommendations.

Additional care will depend on the severity of the psychiatric condition and the health care resources available to the client. The fewer the monetary resources of the client, the greater the access barriers that exist for the most suitable form of treatment.

Clinical Application

A few clinical examples detailing the effect of external enabling factors on disposition plans will be presented. We will address some of the internal variables, as well as the role of the clinician in facilitating compliance with treatment recommendations.

Clinical Example 7-1

The client is a 25-year-old black male who presents to the emergency service requesting medication for the side effects of his neuroleptic medication. He has been in treatment at a local mental health clinic for years and is diagnosed as a chronic paranoid schizophrenic. On admission he is cooperative, casually dressed, and appears "stiff" from his medication. From the history, it seems that he is taking injectable Prolixin on a weekly basis. He does not know the exact dose. He is also taking Benadryl for the side effects. This regimen has existed for several years. His last hospitalization was 18 months ago at the state hospital. He has no complaints of psychotic symptoms, but has a rather constricted life-style.

The problem that this case represents is twofold. First, this client is already in treatment at another setting and seems fairly well established there. Second, it is difficult to determine the reason for his seeking care at the emergency service, since he might just as easily have gone to the mental health clinic. His symptoms are not exaggerated, that is, he is not experiencing an acute dystonic reaction to the medication.

Since the clinician was well acquainted with the clinic staff and their type of setting, she knew that this particular clinic was easily accessible for clients between appointments and was conveniently located in the area where the client lived. After obtaining permission from the client to contact the clinic staff, she learned that this client was becoming dissatisfied with his medication and wanted "extra" medication for its side effects. The dose of medication he was receiving was indeed high, and he began to feel more side effects as he attempted to live a more active life.

After conferring with the clinic staff, the clinician agreed to send the client via taxi to his own clinic, where he could talk to the psychiatrist about his medication.

This situation recurred three more times during the following week. Each time, the staff at the clinic was contacted and the client was returned there for an immediate appointment. It wasn't until the third appointment that we learned that the client had been arriving at the emergency service early enough in the morning to be given breakfast by the nursing staff. Once his breakfasts were discontinued, his visits to the emergency service stopped.

This case illustrates the need for close working relationships with emergency room and clinic staffs, and knowledge about the kinds of services offered by particular clinics. Without an agreeable clinic staff who would see the client immediately and evaluate his side effects, there was likely to be confusion about the medication regimen. Offering this client more medication would not have disrupted his mental status, but it could have lessened the relationship with the clinic and interfered with their overall medication plans.

External enabling factors helped the emergency room staff link this client with his primary treatment setting. The client's social network was not required in this case, largely because the professional support network was responsive and there were resources available to reduce access barriers. The client was already well connected with a clinic (and its staff), which responded quickly to the client's behavior. Monetary resources in the emergency service provided taxi fare to ensure the client's return to the clinic.

Clinical Example 7–2

The client is a 21-year-old black female brought to the emergency service by her parents. She has been behaving strangely for several weeks. This past evening, she removed her clothing and was found wandering in the streets by the local police. Her family reports that she has become increasingly disturbed since her boyfriend left her. They thought she might be experiencing a religious crisis, and therefore had the minister come to the house to bless her. She is regularly employed at a local bookkeeping service but has been unable to work for several weeks. Her job is about to be terminated if she does not return to work soon.

This client's network had been actively involved with her for several weeks while her behavior deteriorated. These persons assessed the client's behavior as a religious crisis, and elected to use the church for care rather than the mental health system. Their lay evaluation resulted in the avoidance of psychiatric care for several weeks.

At the time of the emergency visit, the clinician attempted to have the client admitted to the inpatient psychiatric service. There were no beds available, and the family was told that the client would have to go to the state hospital for care. They objected to that arrangement and agreed to take the client home. They were instructed to call back in a few days to complete the admission procedure.

The family failed to comply with this instruction, and the client was again brought to the emergency service three weeks later by the police. She had again been found wandering naked, and was yelling at passersby on the street. By the time of this second admission, the client had lost her job and her insurance benefits to pay for hospitalization. She was committed by the police and transferred to the state hospital for care.

This situation typifies the importance of understanding the social network's values and the degree of cooperation likely to be forthcoming. During the first admission to the emergency service, several clues existed which would have predicted the family's ambivalence about psychiatric care and their preference for a religious attribution of the problem. There was evidently not enough education from the staff about the client's behavior to sway the family from their convictions and secure psychiatric care. The consequences of this action were severe. The client lost her job and the insurance benefits which might have enabled her to be treated in a setting more of her choosing.

Although the family *politely* agreed to the plan at the time of the first visit, they were nonetheless still convinced of the correctness of *their* assessment of the problem. More aggressive attempts by the staff might have averted the second visit. A staff member could have called the family the next day to inquire about the client's behavior. A home visit would also place the staff in a better position to discuss the situation with the family and continue to reinforce the need for care on an inpatient basis. These outreach services are beneficial for clients (and social network systems) in that they attach the client to the emergency service and attempt treatment on a temporary outpatient basis. Treatment need not always focus directly on the client, but in this case it would have met the needs of the family, which were essential in getting the client into treatment. In this case, the family was in great need of education and working through the idea of their daughter's becoming identified as a mental patient.

Clinical Example 7-3

The client is an 85-year-old female brought to the emergency service by the local police. They were called by neighbors who had witnessed the woman wandering the streets yelling "help me, help me." Her family, a daughter, accompanied the police to the emergency service. At the time of the interview, the client was casually dressed, fairly clean, and somewhat frightened and bewildered by the experience. She was not oriented to time or place, but knew her name and address. The daughter noted that the woman had been living in her own home with her husband, and care was provided on a part-time basis by a home health aide. She knew her mother was sometimes confused but usually able to handle her daily affairs without significant problems. The daughter was adamantly opposed to her mother's being admitted to the hospital and agreed to watch her more closely.

In this case, the family explicitly refused psychiatric care for a member who is probably demented and unable to act in her own behalf. The reasons for the refusal are unclear, but one guesses that there are other hidden agendas that were not disclosed during the interview. Since the client is not an immediate danger to herself, and has a place to live and potential care from an outside resource, there is little the staff can do to bring her into treatment. She does not meet the criteria for dangerousness to self or others since the family has assumed responsibility for her and has agreed to watch her at home.

Later in the day, the client's grandson called the emergency service to find out what had happened. During the conversation, we learned that there had been many family struggles about how to care for this elderly couple. The grandson had wanted more care provided in the home, but his aunt had refused. The family home and the financial expenditures were evidently at the core of this conflict. Thus, it became clearer to the staff what some of the hidden agenda might have been in this case. The arrival of the police and the deteriorating course of this woman's mental condition had almost caused a family crisis. Obviously, the need to maintain the family dynamics outweighed the need for care in this case.

Summary

External variables consist of the social network, access barriers, and demographic data. These variables are independent of the client, but they interact with the client's situation to enable or deter access to mental health resources. At the time of contact with the mental health care system, the variables are fixed, and may or may not provide the client with the necessary range of services needed to solve the immediate crisis.

There are numerous possibilities for molding these factors into an acceptable treatment plan. In some cases, the family network may require education/socialization about the need for care. In others, secondary treatment settings may need information in order to prioritize care for the client. Obtaining an outpatient appointment for the client or arranging for admission to the hospital becomes the responsibility of the clinician. This reduces the burden on the client (and the family) and ensures greater cooperation with a treatment plan.

In order to ensure follow-up care, the clinician, client, social network, and treatment system must agree on the need for care, the type of care, and the time period in which care must be delivered. Access barriers should be revealed at this point in the interview. This allows the client to understand the existing treatment options, and the clinician to predict the likelihood of compliance with a predetermined plan. Without an agreement between client and clinician, compliance is likely to fail. The responsibility for ensuring compliance must reside with the clinician, who has access to systems' variables and treatment options and can therefore arrange a plan of care that is consistent with the client's needs and resources for obtaining desirable care.

References

1. Becker, M., and Maiman, L.: Models of health-related behavior. In: Mechanic, D. (ed.), *Handbook of Health, Health Care, and the Health Professional*. New York: Free Press, pp. 539–568, 1983.

2. Ibid.

3. Hammer, M.; Makiesky-Barrow, S.; and Gutwirth, L.: Social networks and schizophrenia. *Schizophrenia Bulletin, 4,* 522–545, 1978.

4. Ellison, E. S.: Social networks and the mental health caregiving system: Implications for psychiatric nursing practice. *Journal of Psychosocial Nursing and Mental Health Services, 21,* 18–24, 1983.

5. Norbeck, J. S.: The use of social support in clinical practice. *Journal of Psychosocial Nursing and Mental Health Services, 20,* 22–29, 1982.

6. Ibid.

7. Cochran, M. M., and Brassard, J. N.: Child development and personal social networks. *Child Development, 50,* 601–616, 1979.

8. Zonana, H.; Henisz, J.; and Levine, M.: Psychiatric emergency services a decade later. *Psychiatry in Medicine, 4,* 273–290, 1973.

9. Faas, M., and Elstun, N.: Psychiatric emergency service: A growing
specialty. *Journal of Psychiatric Nursing and Mental Health Services,
17,* 13–19, 1979.

10. Becker and Maiman, op. cit.

11. Howes, E.; Levy, J.; Luongo, S.; and Monteleone, M.: A team approach to emergency psychiatry. *Journal of Psychiatric Nursing and
Mental Health Services, 17,* 31–37, 1979.

CHAPTER 8

ADHERENCE

Compliance or adherence implies cooperation by the client in following treatment suggestions designed by the clinician. The concept of compliance has been criticized for its unidirectional expectation that clients will follow prescribed care plans regardless of their ability, interest, or willingness. The assumption has been that achievement of health care benefits will outweigh all other competing forces in the client's life in order to ensure compliance. When clients fail to comply with treatment recommendations, blame is placed on them, with a tendency to label noncompliant behavior as indicative of poor motivation or self-destructiveness.

The two previous chapters, on internal and external enabling variables, provided a foundation for understanding the *client's* perspective in health care decision making. The interaction between the client's interests and needs and the resources of the health care system is the basis for negotiating treatment recommendations.

The overriding philosophy of this chapter is that adherence is more likely to occur under circumstances of client involvement, as opposed to assigning clients arbitrarily to treatment settings that are appropriate for care but are not consistent with the belief system of the client. When negotiating treatment plans, the clinician should attempt to extend the empathy inherent in understanding the nature of the client's problem to the process of deciding which treatment plans most effectively meet the client's needs. The concept of negotiation is consistent with a nursing philosophy which attends to the client's perspective in designing care plans. Without client involvement, care plans may be psychiatrically sound but fail to integrate client motivation, understanding of the need for care, and ability to carry out the care plan. Additionally, the client's resources necessary to purchase the elements of the treatment plan (e.g., medication, transportation, insurance) must be defined before devising treatments in order to avoid unrealistic expectations of clients.

In this chapter, we will elaborate on the framework for negotiation as conceptualized by Lazare and his associates.[1,2] Their models of the customer approach and negotiated adherence succinctly describe the need to attend to the client's perspective and engage in discussions on how best to plan care that is acceptable to him or her. We will also review the existing data on known patterns of compliance in psychiatric emergency services which demonstrate unique problems for this high-risk population, who by their presence in the emergency service seem eager for care, yet who frequently fail to comply with treatment recommendations of staff.

Clinical Content

Overview

Compliance is defined as "the extent to which a person's behavior coincides with medical advice."[3] This definition places the responsibility for following medical regimens on the client. *Adherence* denotes attachment, devotion, or agreement. This term is more frequently used in the literature to deemphasize the exclusive burden of responsibility on the client. *Adherence* is used in place of *compliance* to imply varying degrees of cooperation with treatment plans and prediction of adherence by sharing the responsibility between the clinician and the client in arriving at mutually agreed upon health care practices.

The mental health literature has emphasized *adherence* since therapeutic communication is a fundamental issue in mental health care. Conversely, psychiatry is one of the few specialties in which care is legally enforced through commitment. Thus, in actual clinical practice, both ends of the continuum are represented: negotiation of choices and tolerance for individual differences, and commitment of clients to treatment in selected settings by the courts. In the final analysis, the right to participate in treatment decisions is reserved for those clients able to make reasonable decisions about health care practices or those unlikely to experience immediately grave consequences if they do not follow prescribed treatment recommendations.

Eliciting cooperation from the client is essential in attempting to provide care on a *voluntary* basis. At a minimum, the client should be invited to contribute to the care plan even when care is initially involuntary. For long-term or outpatient care, negotiating alternative experiences for clients is a necessary part of adherence, whereby client and clinician agree on the best resource and method of obtaining care.

Common conflicts in adherence are the result of disagreement over:

the problem
the goals of treatment
the methods of treatment
the conditions of treatment, or
the clinician–patient relationship[4]

These conflicts represent many of the internal and external variables associated with enabling conditions. Client and clinician must agree on the problem and the best method of treatment in order to arrive at a mutually agreed upon plan. If conditions of treatment are not acceptable secondary to insufficient resources on the part of the client or the community, the value accorded the treatment resource will diminish. The relationship established during the psychiatric emergency visit will become a *model* for clients' expectations of future therapeutic relationships. Without the development of positive transference, clients may become reluctant to seek additional care.

Compliance in Psychiatric Patient Populations

Studies of follow-up rates from the emergency service have noted that only 30 to 50% of clients complete appointments at secondary treatment settings.[5] This is an alarmingly low rate of follow-up for clients who approached the emergency service and probably had significant emotional concerns which prompted them to seek care. The high rate of repeater clients, 14% of the psychiatric emergency population, indicates that many of these clients are in states of chronic emotional distress or have chronic mental conditions necessitating ongoing psychiatric care.[6]

Many of these studies have utilized demographic variables in order to predict compliance. Unfortunately, the only demographic variable consistently associated with poor compliance is lower socioeconomic status.[7,8] Age, gender, marital status, religion, and education have had little predictive value in determining who completes a referral.[9,10] The predictive value of lower socioeconomic status may be related to access barriers which prevent clients from obtaining services secondary to isolation and limited resources. An alternate explanation might be the tendency for lower socioeconomic clients to utilize services on an emergency basis rather than make long-range plans for continued utilization. Again, the reduced access barriers of the emergency service may attract clients who prefer to use immediately available services and are less likely to value continued, long-term treatment.

The emergency room psychiatric population has been described as high risk, as evidenced by increased rates of previous treatment, high mobility, and isolation in their life-styles.[11] These characteristics reduce the commitment to long-term care and the capacity to tolerate the constraints of planned approaches which provide long-range benefits rather than short-term relief from psychological problems.

One characteristic of clients known to affect compliance is hopelessness/helplessness. Follow-through with discharge plans has been positively related to higher scores on hopelessness/helplessness scales.[12] This finding supports Jerome Frank's statement that demoralization is necessary to involve oneself in psychotherapy.[13] In a similar vein, Tolsdorf found psychotics to be less likely to ask for support from their social milieu, believing it to be useless, impossible, or potentially dangerous.[14] The relationship between demoralization and compliance is probably curvilinear, that is, either too much or too little interferes with completion of referrals.

Diagnostic variables have also been examined for their role in compliance. Drug and alcohol problems are more often linked to poor follow-through. This may be related in part to the denial associated with addictive disorders. The clinical interview may not begin to address the magnitude of denial, and thus referrals reflect recommendations for obvious treatment resources in the community rather than the client's *actual* willingness to engage in treatment. These clients also have coexistent personality disorders which are associated with insufficient motivation and insight necessary to begin treatment.

Depression has been related to both good and poor compliance.[15,16] The reasoning behind this finding is unclear, but may be the curvilinear relationship between demoralization and adherence. Relief obtained during the emergency visit may reduce the impetus to seek additional care. Another factor related to this diagnosis may be the number of administrative barriers required to complete the referral. Clients with moderate to severe symptomatology are unable to tolerate the delays, repeated contacts, and paperwork necessary to enter new systems.

The interaction between psychotic diagnoses and age has shown that clients over the age of 30 tend to stay in treatment longer, whereas younger ones prefer brief treatment.[17] One explanation for this may be the socialization process that occurs once clients value treatment and become more attached to mental health care systems. Before this occurs, clients seek care only when symptoms are severe or social functioning has significantly deteriorated.

Interaction Model of Adherence

The model of Lazare and his associates began with the concept of the client as a customer.[18] In their first attempt to identify the needs of the client in seeking care, they successfully shifted the clinician's attention toward the agendas clients brought with them during the help-seeking process. Table 8–1 lists the requests they categorized from clients in a walk-in mental health clinic.[19] The mere documentation of these requests lends support to the idea that clients have preconceived requests for help that extend beyond symptom relief, and are too sophisticated merely to accept the type of care designed by the health care provider.

For comparison purposes, we have added a complementary list of clinicians' services likely to be provided during psychiatric emergency care. Numbers which correspond with clinician services and client need are listed in parentheses next to each client request. As the table demonstrates, there are usually several services for each client request. The clinician actually provides multiple functions in the emergency service which may or may not be needed or valued by every client. Thus, it is important to attempt to match the clinician's service with the client's requests before designing a treatment plan that is below or beyond the client's actual needs.

Negotiating adherence to the treatment plan is analogous to providing therapy. Timing the inquiry about the client's agenda is criti-

TABLE 8-1   Clients' Requests versus Clinicians' Resources

CLIENT	CLINICIAN
Administrative request (7,9)	1. Assessment and evaluation
Advice (5,6)	2. Diagnosis (psychiatric/medical)
Clarification [of the problem] (1,2)	3. Empathy
Community triage (7)	4. Insight
Confession (3)	5. Advice
Control (6,9)	6. Therapeutic interventions
Medical help (2,8)	7. Referral to settings
Psychological expertise (1)	8. Medication
Psychodynamic insight (4)	9. Legal—commitment, welfare,
Reality contact (4,6)	disability
Social intervention (6,7)	
Succor (3,5)	
Ventilation (3)	
Nothing	

Source: Adapted from Lazare, A. (ed.): *Outpatient Psychiatry.* Baltimore: Williams and Wilkins, 1979, pp. 143–144.

cal. The clinician must avoid premature questioning which might be conceived as provocative by the client. If the first question is "What do you want?", the client may feel a lack of interest in his or her problem. At the other extreme, it is often too late to discuss alternatives if the clinician has already suggested a plan and the client does not feel invited to participate in the discussion of alternatives. Lazare and Eisenthal suggest listening to a description of the problem and then inquiring about the "meaning of the problem" for the client before discussing the client's agenda for care.[20] This serves as a lead-in to the discussion of what the client thinks would be most helpful in using the emergency service for care.

One study of medical clients who appeared at the emergency service for care noted that before clients were able to seek care, they had to have made a provisional diagnosis of their problem in order to select the most appropriate system for treatment.[21] Thus, clients *also* engage in a process of self-diagnosis.

If the client's agenda for care and the clinician's assessment of the problem match, there is little problem in defining the treatment plan. This is, of course, the best of all possible situations. As noted earlier, conflict may arise over the problem, method of treatment, goals, conditions, or the therapist–client relationship. When any of these circumstances become the issue, adherence is likely to be compromised unless the conflict is resolved.

The clinician *must* be the person responsible for determining that conflict has occurred. Clients often give multiple clues that they are dissatisfied or unable to follow through, but these must be appropriately interpreted by the clinician. Inviting the client to share his or her agenda for care is the first step, with subsequent steps providing the atmosphere necessary for clients to believe that they will be able to share their ideas and not be dismissed or ridiculed by the clinician.

Differences in opinion between client and clinician can be resolved at several levels. From the clinician's standpoint, the client's safety (or that of society) is always a prime consideration. Is it safe for the client to disregard the clinician's plan? If it is safe, can care be provided in a less restrictive setting? These issues prevent the clinician from assigning total responsibility to the client who may be incapable of deciding the safest care plan. Beyond the legal/moral decision, a wide range of options is possible in order to give the client maximal control over the treatment plan while staying within the margin of safety required to treat the immediate problem adequately.

Negotiation simply moves the clinical interview into a therapeutic mode in which the clinician gains a greater understanding of the client's needs for therapy, which may differ from those determined by the clinician. For example, the client may be interested only in a crisis approach to the problem, although it is clear to the clinician that there are multiple problems that could benefit from long-range therapeutic intervention. This discrepancy in goals must be resolved by the client or the treatment arena where the client receives care. For example, the case presented in Clinical Example 1–1, in which a young man with chronic paranoid symptoms approached the emergency service for help only when his symptoms increased, but was unwilling to seek long-term care in an outpatient setting, demonstrated restraint by the clinician in not withholding care to a client who is resistant to organized mental health care systems and does not present an immediate danger to himself or others.

Some clients' requests are for services other than direct therapy, as noted in Table 8–1. Nonclinical requests may be more difficult to elicit, since the client may not feel comfortable asking for nontherapeutic services (e.g., disability statements for welfare, Social Security evaluations, phone calls to therapists). In these situations, the clinician may note that there seems to be a hidden agenda that is not immediately obvious.[22]

Hidden agendas are most easily noted when the story does not correspond to the behavior presented or the client does not seem particularly interested in or satisfied with the process by which care is being arranged in the emergency service.[23] These ulterior motives can be misinterpreted as resistance unless the clinician is sensitive to clients who utilize health care services for other than health care needs.

Once the client's request emerges, the process of negotiation gets underway. Whether or not the clinician feels able to fulfill the request, it is important to continue the discussion until the request is clear both in the client's and the clinician's minds. The clinician must resist the temptation to become defensive or anxious when it appears that the request cannot be fulfilled or is unrealistic. Negotiation requires *both partners* to give and take in order to arrive at a mutually agreeable treatment plan.

In some cases, the client may need additional information about *why* the clinician has suggested a particular therapy or setting for continued care. This provides an opportunity to socialize the client or dispel myths the client may have about treatment. The adversarial component of negotiation must also be tempered. Clients are rarely negativistic about future care because of some aggressive stance; instead, they have their own agendas for care which may seem peculiar to the clinician.

Figure 8–1 describes one process of negotiation between client and clinician. The respective phases are listed in the paradigm. Phase one describes the *need* for care. The client determines need based on subjective symptoms/signs, the degree of threat, and the meaning of the symptoms based on knowledge or past experience. If insight or cognitive processes are diminished, the lay evaluation system may have initiated the health care contact. Validation of need is the responsibility of the clinician. This is accomplished by the clinical interview, the psychiatric history, and the MSE. The *process* in Phase One is the amount of agreement between client and clinician about the nature and severity of the clinical problem.

Once the clinical problem has been identified, Phase Two (Resources) focuses on those factors which identify the most likely resources to be valued. The client's use of resources will be determined by his or her motivation (i.e., perceived susceptibility to the problem and the seriousness of the symptoms), evaluation of health care services, and resources/barriers to care. The clinician is also selecting resources during this process, depending on a knowledge of what is available, the type of service delivered, and the accessibility of the client and clinician to the resource. This phase actually begins the negotiation process in that the clinician hopes to understand better the *match* between the client's problem and his or her previous experience with care which will predict future use patterns and the existing community resources that might be appropriate for care.

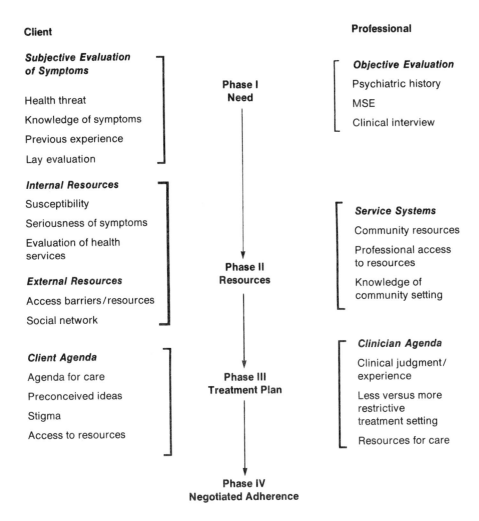

Figure 8-1   Paradigm of negotiated adherence.

During Phase Three, the amount of negotiation required will be determined by the proximity of the clinician's plan and the client's agenda. The greater the agreement between the two, the less negotiation is required. Clients' agendas for care is elicited at this time. It may reflect previous experience with care, preconceived ideas about treatment, and the amount of stigma associated with psychiatric care. Knowledge of their own resources for care may also determine their preferences, particularly when they know care will provided in publicly financed settings. Clinicians will determine their agenda for care based on a clinical judgment about the *type* of care needed, the amount of restrictiveness required to deliver safe care, and the community settings available for care.

Phase Four lists the factors which must be addressed in negotiating safe, acceptable care. The clinician negotiates on the basis of safety, reducing access barriers to settings, and limiting treatment goals to immediate problems. Clients negotiate on the basis of limited resources for care, individualized treatment plans, and increased access to agencies. The client is expected to take some responsibility in entering health care systems, whereas the clinician attempts to reduce administrative barriers.

The value of exploring the client's requests/agendas for care is threefold:

1. Diagnostic value
2. Enhancement of a therapeutic interaction
3. Collaborative nature and mutuality[24]

Thus, the clinician facilitates an atmosphere of joint planning with the client and gains additional information that is useful diagnostically. The *congruence* or *vagueness* of the client's request is important in predicting compliance, but it also defines the degree of cognitive impairment secondary to organic or psychiatric disorders.[25] The overall value of understanding the client's needs and agendas for care is its demonstration of respect for and interest in the client as a unique, separate human being. The ability to deliver comprehensive care is dependent on the rapport and understanding displayed toward the client. Even though an emergency visit may not result in total adherence to the treatment plan, it is hoped that the client is somewhat better off for the interaction with the clinician.

Negotiation with Health Care Settings

The burden of negotiating should *not* reside exclusively with the client. Substantial work is done by the emergency service in reducing the administrative barriers that occur when clients enter treatment settings. These efforts originate with clinicians, who note the obvious problems in securing appointments or admissions to community settings which prevent easy access for clients.

The most common approach used to increase compliance is to have the emergency room therapist make the first appointment and reduce the waiting time before the first appointment.[26,27] Compliance rates almost doubled in these studies when this action was taken. Depressed clients were particularly helped by having the first appointment made for them,[28] whereas neurotic or character-disordered clients responded better to shorter waiting times.[29]

One inpatient treatment setting has utilized a "referral coordinator" to facilitate completion of outpatient care for discharged clients.[30] In a three-phase study, the authors found that compliance rates increased from 35.3 to 75.6%. The major functions of the referral coordinator included:

Attendance at staff meetings for case finding
Sharing information about community resources
Meeting with the patient to discuss discharge planning
Making an appointment for the client
Contacting the client before discharge as a reminder

Adopting standards for referrals from the emergency service is an important aspect of the therapist's role in that setting. The combined problems of reduced access to settings and high levels of psychopathology militate against completed referrals to treatment settings with complicated administrative procedures. Apart from the negotiation between client and clinician during a clinical encounter, the staff need to establish relationships with community agencies that allow them access for their clients, keep them informed of policy/procedural changes that affect intake and referral, and let them know about availability of resources. Up-to-date knowledge about appointments, bed availability, and new programs prevents the burden of responsibility from falling on an already compromised client.

The clinician negotiates with clinical agencies in an effort to prioritize care for emergency service clients, and in turn becomes a resource for the community in screening and treating psychiatric emergency situations that arise elsewhere. This exchange of services is one way of increasing the community network of psychiatric services with the goal of maximizing the use of limited mental health resources.

Designing Treatment Plans

The interactional model presented demonstrates the need to reduce the complexity of follow-up care (e.g., making the first appointment, reducing the waiting time, capitalizing on clients' motivation for care by understanding their agenda). The follow-up care is dependent on:

    The clinical problem
    The safest setting for care
    The least restrictive setting for care
    The client's willingness to seek care in that setting
    The client's eligibility to receive care
    The availability of services from that resource

The clinician's decision-making process is dependent on the configuration of these factors, which will determine the overall likelihood of increased adherence with the plan.

Thus, the clinician must rely on a balance of clinical judgment, knowledge of external and internal enabling factors, and common sense. Understanding the client's unique background with respect to psychiatric care utilization provides a foundation for adding diagnostic and community factors which will enhance or decrease adherence.

Services Designed to Improve Adherence

In order to improve adherence with follow-up care, psychiatric emergency staffs have designed their own programs for clients who do not seem to be appropriate candidates for existing programs. These were reviewed in Chapter 1, but will be highlighted here since they are frequently an alternative resource for clients. The common alternative resources are:

    Holding beds
    Outreach visits
    Return appointments at the emergency service[31]

These services provide intermediate care that is less restrictive than inpatient services but more engaging than outpatient care.

These services extend emergency care to clients who are not eligible for or capable of complying with organized mental health programs. Outreach services have long been identified as an ideal role for nurses, who could make home visits to determine why clients did not keep follow-up appointments at a mental health clinic.[32] Similarly, holding beds in the emergency service allow clients to be maintained safely until a bed becomes available in an inpatient setting. This reduces the burden on the family to care for an acutely disturbed member and allows clients to receive care in settings they prefer.

The social support system of the client is more likely to become involved in treatment issues with these extended services. Education of family members can be accomplished more easily during follow-up appointments or during outreach visits by staff members. This avoids communication breakdowns and provides a readily available resource for the family of a disturbed person.

Adherence is positively influenced by understanding the client's agenda for care and preconceived ideas about treatment, as well as the willingness of the clinician to engage with clients and their support system to effect follow-up treatment in the most valued setting. Failure to elicit an agenda or understand the client's needs for care (which often differ significantly from their clinical problems) will predict communication deficits in the client–clinician interaction. It is these deficits that prevent health care providers from understanding the likelihood of adherence and methods which might improve it. The factors which make adherence more or less likely are presented in Table 8–2. This includes known circumstances which facilitate or impede attachment to psychiatric care plans.

TABLE 8–2   Factors Related to Adherence to Treatment Plans

ADHERENCE MORE LIKELY	ADHERENCE LESS LIKELY
Middle to upper socioeconomic class	Lower socioeconomic status; diagnoses that carry a high degree of cognitive impairment
Clients who are able to make a request of the clinician	Clients who possess diminished contact with reality
A moderately high level of helplessness/hopelessness: a sense of demoralization	Extremes of this factor in either direction
Motivation	Absence of motivation
Behavior related to adherence is valued by the client	Behavior related to adherence not valued by the client
A perception that the recommended treatment will produce the desired outcome	Absence of this perception
High susceptibility and seriousness perceived by the client	Low susceptibility and seriousness perceived by the client
High feasibility and self-efficacy perceived by the client	Low feasibility and self-efficacy perceived by the client
Client's perspective carefully attended to by the clinician	Client's perspective not attended to by the clinician
Minimal discrepancy between client's agenda and clinician's recommendation	Substantial discrepancy between client's agenda and clinician's recommendation
Use of a negotiated approach	Client's request and expectation is not made explicit and then used as a basis for negotiation

TABLE 8–2   continued

ADHERENCE MORE LIKELY	ADHERENCE LESS LIKELY
The client perceives the clinician as genuinely helpful	The clinician is not perceived as helpful
A collaborative spirit is achieved	A collaborative spirit is not achieved
The clinician contacts the recovery agency and makes an appointment	The name of an agency is provided as a referral
An appointment is made soon after the emergency	The appointment time is long after the perceived emergency
The clinician seeing the client on follow-up is made known to the client	The client is given an appointment with an agency but does not know the clinician
The clinician in the referring agency makes contact with the client prior to the first visit	The client is left to initiate contact

Clinical Application

In this section, we will present case examples of difficult disposition plans requiring alternate planning and negotiated adherence with clients. The emergency service is frequently without an exhaustive list of treatment resources and therefore must find or create alternative solutions.

Clinical Example 8–1

The client is a 34-year-old white, divorced female who arrives at the emergency service requesting admission to the hospital. She has been increasingly depressed and frustrated with her life. There are no immediate crises, but the client has experienced increased insomnia (early morning awakening), a 5-pound weight loss, and anorexia. She has been in treatment before at a local mental health clinic and has had two previous admissions, one in the local crisis service and the other at the state hospital. She fears that she may become suicidal if she is not admitted, and has not been in outpatient treatment which would give her access to the local mental health clinic. The client is not working, and supports herself and her 6-year-old daughter on welfare. Other pertinent clinical data include her lack of friends and few interests outside her home. She has not been suicidal in the past, but rates her mood as 2 on a scale of 1 to 10 (10 being the best she ever felt).

This client is somewhat difficult to evaluate in terms of her immediate danger. She does not have a plan, although she has some of the symptoms of depression (e.g., weight loss, insomnia, and mood changes). Her request for care is straightforward; she wants to be admitted to the hospital. It is not clear that she would pose a threat to herself or others, but there are also only a few community resources in the area that would be able to see her for care, and this would be after some delay in arranging for an appointment since the community mental health clinic has a waiting list.

After discussing the situation further with the client, it seemed clear that she was in some distress, although she was unable to identify any particular stressors. She was informed that the beds on the crisis unit were full, and that if she wanted to be admitted, she would have to go to the state hospital. At this point she became extremely angry, telling us how awful her last stay was and that she would *never* return there for care voluntarily.

The next phase of the discussion focused on alternative methods of treatment. She could be given the number of the mental health clinic, and we would contact them to arrange for an appointment as soon as possible, or she could maintain contact with the emergency service staff and return for brief follow-up with us.

The client was not interested in any of these alternatives, again persisting in her demand for admission. Since she was receiving welfare assistance, we thought she might have some days left on her policy for inpatient care. (Welfare coverage usually allows for 30 days of hospitalization a year.) A call to the local welfare office verified that she did have 10 days left on this year's allotment of hospitalization. After this information was shared with the client, she stated that she would like to use her remaining days now. We arranged for her to be admitted to one of the private psychiatric hospitals in the area. She was informed that it was possible that she would be discharged at the end of 10 days, and this was agreeable to her.

Although we were finally able to meet this client's request for care, there was little opportunity to negotiate with her. She remained steadfast in her request for inpatient care, which was not totally unreasonable even though her depressive symptoms were not severe. Had she not had access to 10 days of inpatient coverage through her welfare policy, we would have been better able to negotiate with her once her options became limited.

The next case demonstrates the need to obtain support from the family system in order to convince a client to receive care.

Clinical Example 8–2

The client is a 30-year-old white, single female who resides with her parents and a sister in the family home. The family has brought her in for care, against her will, because of her strange behavior at home. During the interview with the client, she was guarded but pleasant in giving minimal answers to our questions. She denied having any emotional problems, but did acknowledge another psychiatric hospitalization a few years ago. She did not see any reason to be admitted at this time, but was not resentful or angry toward her family for bringing her to the hospital. Her affect was contricted, but not flat. She did not appear to be hallucinating and would not disclose any unusual ideation. The most obvious problem seemed to be the family's concern and this woman's rather bland response to being brought to the hospital against her will.

This situation is problematic in that the family is requesting care, not the client. The severity of the client's symptoms would not warrant involuntary treatment. One simplistic, although less humanitarian approach would be denial of admission on the grounds that she does not meet the criteria for involuntary care and is not willing to sign in voluntarily. This would clearly not meet the stated request of the family to have the client admitted.

Although the objective clinical data arouse suspicion about the client's mental status, the family is the prime informant about her psychopathological symptoms. They are also beginning to tire of caring for the client, which may herald a crisis in the near future if interventions do not occur now. At this time, the clinician must determine the need for interventions for the family or devise strategies for the client *and* the family.

After discussing options with the family, it seemed clear that they were unwilling to tolerate much more of the client's behavior. They were also resistant to the idea of taking the client to a mental health clinic in the hope that she would agree to become an outpatient. Thus, we mutually agreed to talk with the client and her family together, with the following goals in mind:

> Share the family's perspective about her behavior and how this distressed them

Have the family clearly define their limits in continuing to care
for her in her current state

Attempt to talk the client into admitting herself voluntarily to
the crisis unit until her problems could be clarified

The emergency room psychiatric staff, the family, and the client
met for about half an hour to discuss these points. Not until the client was able to understand the family's frustration with her and their
limited ability to continue to care for her did she finally agree to admit herself voluntarily to the service. Her paranoid symptoms were
more obvious during this family meeting, lending further support to
the family's original concern. The client was admitted to the crisis
unit without incident, started on neuroleptic medication, and returned home within 10 days. Her follow-up at a local mental health
clinic was arranged prior to discharge, and the family agreed to have
her return home.

Summary

This chapter has discussed adherence as an interaction between client
and clinician. The motivating forces in clients' lives that cause them
to seek care may be very different from those required to stay in
treatment following the initial contact with the health care provider.
Therefore, the emergency room clinician must determine what motivated the client to seek care and what will be important in facilitating
the client's entry into secondary care systems.

The act of referring a client for continued care entails more than
supplying the client with a phone number and address. During an
emotional state severe enough to bring the client to the emergency
service, it seems unlikely that the client will have the emotional resources to comply with a complicated follow-up plan. Experience
with many treatment settings documents the lengthy administrative
process required for admission. Understanding these administrative
barriers can provide the clinician with opportunities to bypass them
whenever possible or to refer clients to settings where they can be easily registered for care.

Designing treatment programs within the emergency service
which offer intermediate care is one method of simplifying care for
clients who are not yet eligible for existing treatment settings. This
includes clients in crisis who need more immediate outpatient care
than an appointment in the distant future, or clients who could bene-

fit from a one- or two-day inpatient stay but do not meet the full criteria for admission to an inpatient setting.

Negotiating adherence is one method of planning intervention strategies jointly by the client and clinician. Shifting the clinical interview away from assessment and toward care planning expands the resources of the emergency service and, it is hoped, strengthens the client's link with secondary treatment settings.

References

1. Lazare, A.; Eisenthal, S.; and Wasserman, L.: The customer approach to patienthood. *Archives of General Psychiatry, 32,* 553–558, 1975.

2. Eisenthal, S.; Emery, R.; Lazare, A.; and Udlin, H.: Adherence and the negotiated approach to patienthood. *Archives of General Psychiatry, 36,* 393–398, 1979.

3. Haynes, R. B.; Taylor, D. W.; and Sackett, D. C. (eds.): *Compliance in health care.* Baltimore: Johns Hopkins University Press, pp. 1–2, 1979.

4. Lazare, A.; Eisenthal, S.; and Frank, A.: A negotiated approach to the clinical encounter. II. Conflict and negotiation. In: Lazare, A. (ed.): *Oupatient Psychiatry.* Baltimore: Williams & Wilkins, pp. 157–171, 1979.

5. Rogawski, A. S., and Edmundson, B.: Factors affecting the outcome of psychiatric interagency referral. *American Journal of Psychiatry, 127,* 925–934, 1977.

6. Raphling, D. L., and Lion, J.: Patients with repeated admissions to a psychiatric emergency service. *Community Mental Health Journal, 6,* 313–318, 1970.

7. Eisenthal et al., op. cit.

8. Hoenig, J., and Ragg, N.: The non-attending psychiatric outpatient: An administrative problem. *Medical Care, 4,* 96–100, 1966.

9. Eisenthal et al., op. cit.

10. Rogawski and Edmundson, op. cit.

11. Huffine, C. L., and Craig, I. J.: Catchment and community. *Archives of General Psychiatry, 28,* 483–488, 1973.

12. Tessler, R., and Mason, J. H.: Continuity of care in the delivery of mental health services. *American Journal of Psychiatry, 36,* 1297–1301, 1979.

13. Frank, J. E.: *Persuasion and Healing.* Baltimore: Johns Hopkins Press, pp. 134–141, 1961.

14. Tolsdorf, C. C.: Social networks, support, and coping: An exploratory study. *Family Process, 15,* 407–417, 1976.

15. Jellinek, M.: Referrals from a psychiatric emergency room: Relationship of compliance to demographic and interview variables. *American Journal of Psychiatry, 135,* 209–213, 1978.

16. Craig, R. J.; Huffine, C. L.; and Brooks, M.: Completion of referrals to psychiatric services by inner city residents. *Archives of General Psychiatry, 31,* 353–357, 1974.

17. Ibid.

18. Lazare et al. op. cit.

19. Lazare, A., and Eisenthal, S.: A negotiated approach to the clinical encounter. I. Attending to the patient's perspective. In: Lazare, A. (ed.): *Outpatient Psychiatry.* Baltimore: Williams & Wilkins, pp. 141–156, 1979.

20. Ibid.

21. Alonzo, A.: Acute illness behavior: A conceptual exploration and specification. *Social Science and Medicine, 14A,* 515–526, 1980.

22. Barsky, A.: Hidden reasons some patients visit doctors. *Annals of Internal Medicine, 94,* 492–498, 1981.

23. Ibid.

24. Lazare and Eisenthal, op. cit.

25. Jellinek, op. cit.

26. Rogawski and Edmundson, op. cit.

27. Townsend, J. A.: Psychiatric inpatient unit and clinic liaison service. *Journal of Psychiatric and Mental Health Services, 14,* 7–9, 1976.

28. Craig et al., op. cit.

29. Ibid.

30. Bogin, D. L.; Anisk, S.; Traub, H.; and Kline, G.: The effects of a referral coordinator on compliance with psychiatric discharge plans. *Hospital and Community Psychiatry, 35,* 702–706, 1984.

31. Spitz, L.: The evolution of a psychiatric emergency crisis intervention service in a medical emergency room setting. *Comprehensive Psychiatry, 17,* 99–113, 1976.

32. Coleman, J. V., and Dumas, R.: Contributions of a nurse in an adult psychiatric clinic: An exploratory project. *Mental Hygiene, 46,* 448–453, 1962.

CHAPTER 9

DECISION MAKING IN EMERGENCY CARE

The preceding chapters have provided a foundation for the clinical content and examples of psychiatric emergency assessment, risk factors, and adherence. In this chapter, we will attempt to unite the material presented earlier into a conceptual framework that facilitates clinical judgment in planning care for psychiatric emergency clients.

In achieving the goals of psychiatric emergency care, the clinician must match the nature and severity of the client's condition with an appropriate method of treatment in the most satisfactory setting. To a large extent, the clinician often makes these decisions in isolation. There is frequently the sense that the decision is made in a vacuum, with no way of knowing the outcome of the interventions planned. There are very few rules which guide the decision-making process at this level. Agreement between clinicians about diagnosis and intervention plans is often low. This occurs as a result of differing educational programs, clinical and personal experiences, professional identity and emphases, and the stage of professional development.

We have therefore defined some standards of care for the psychiatric emergency service. They are as follows:

Thorough evaluations with attention to multiple hypotheses

An interview process which maximizes client disclosure

Collaboration and consultation with other care providers for verification or validation of care planning

Conscientious attention to legal/ethical issues of treatment in the least restrictive but most appropriate setting

Inclusion of the client and/or social network in the decision-making process whenever possible

Those standards for professional practice are generic to the emergency service and apply to persons of the various disciplines who practice in the emergency room.

The goal of emergency psychiatric care is to maximize a brief contact with the aim of clarifying the client's problem, providing immediate care, or linking the client with treatment settings for continued care. In order to achieve this goal, clinicians must relinquish some of their identity to discipline-specific behavior and adopt a more generic approach to clients in the emergency service. For example, the psychiatric nurse may need to attend to medical problems and psychiatric diagnoses, while practitioners in other disciplines may need to attend to the client's perspective and the *psychosocial* problems which precipitated the health care contact. This blurring of roles, although initially confusing, will eventually lead to clearer definitions of the care requirements in psychiatric emergency services rather than applying traditional techniques to a new setting.

Clinical Content

Decision making in disposition planning at the emergency service has been difficult to standardize secondary to the numerous factors which impinge on the clinician's (and client's) selection of treatment settings. Even when factors are identified which sway clinical decisions, there is rarely a clear indication of appropriate treatment settings. *Diagnosis,* in and of itself, has only partially explained which clients are admitted for care and which ones are referred to outpatient settings. *Severity of suicidal or homicidal behavior* is an additional variable that *may* distinguish those admitted from those given an outpatient referral. This is partially related to the criteria for involuntary care, which allow clinicians to confine mentally ill clients deemed dangerous to themselves or others. Another variable considered in disposition planning has been *adherence.* The client's lack of motivation for care often explains the use of involuntary commitment or the failure to follow through with referral to another setting. Lastly, the array of public and private treatment settings may determine the choice of setting secondary to the client's *access to resources* for care.

Conflicting findings from research studies support the inconsistency of these variables as reliable predictors of intervention planning. One study noted that admissions to an inpatient setting from the emergency service were *more* likely to occur for clients in the following diagnostic categories:

Mania
Schizophrenia
Major depression

Admissions were *less* likely for clients with the following diagnostic problems:

Substance abuse
Adjustment and neurotic disorders
Organic brain syndrome
Personality disorders[1]

Somewhat conflicting results were obtained in another study which noted that schizophrenics had low admission rates, while affective and organic conditions had higher rates.[2]

Table 9–1 lists the admissions, by diagnostic category, to a psychiatric emergency intensive care unit located adjacent to an emergency service.[3] This program provided brief ($\pm$ 72 hours) treatment to clients admitted from the emergency service. As the table indicates, the majority of the admissions were from the major psychiatric diagnostic categories (e.g., schizophrenia and affective disorders), supporting the results of the earlier study, which noted the increased rates of admission for schizophrenic disorders. This would seem to support the use of inpatient care for severely disturbed cli-

TABLE 9–1   Admissions to a Psychiatric Intensive Care Unit

Schizophreniform disorders—50%
Affective disorders with associated suicidal behavior—40%
Severe nonpsychotic anxiety states—4%
Acute brain syndrome (nonalcoholic substance abuse)—3%
Various situational reactions—3%

Source: Adapted from Comstock, B. S.: Psychiatric emergency intensive care. *Psychiatric Clinics of North America, 6,* 305–316, 1983.

ents who might pose a threat to themselves or others without inpatient confinement.

The next factor associated with inpatient care is suicidal and homicidal ideation/threat. In addition to severity of symptoms, which often correlates with diagnostic categories, suicidal and homicidal behavior has been classified as the second most useful predictor of admissions for inpatient care.[4] This study found that one-third of the variance in admissions from the emergency service were accounted for by these two variables: severity of symptoms and suicidal/homicidal ideation. It is not surprising that suicidal or homicidal ideation would be correlated with admission, since these two criteria are most consistently included in commitment statutes for involuntary care.

Resources for care have also been noted to influence the selection of treatment settings by the emergency service. The effect of resources on decision making is often related to the number of alternative services which militate against the use of traditional settings.[5] In other words, systems with access to creative alternatives such as day treatment and home care are less likely to rely exclusively on inpatient settings for treatment of the severely disabled client.

Although there have been conflicting research findings on the reliability of diagnosis, suicidal/homicidal threat, and resource availability in clinical decision making, these are the three most tangible factors to consider in planning emergency care dispositions. Other factors cited as intervening variables in clinical decision making include clinical experience, discipline, age or sex bias of the therapist, and peer pressure.[6] These factors are almost impossible to modify. Therefore, we will focus primarily on the factors previously described (clinical problem/diagnosis, risk factors, and resources).

Characteristics of Treatment Settings

Perhaps a more helpful approach to understanding the use of selected settings is delineation of the capabilities of settings for providing specific *types* of care. There are obvious differences between inpatient and outpatient services, and these may be more helpful in determining which clients are likely to benefit from the particular treatment setting chosen. Friedman has organized a framework which delineates the benefits of inpatient care.[7]

Protection
   Dangerousness which is pervasive and acute

Severe psychopathology with functional impairment and lack
of supports

Disengagement from a stressful environment

Diagnosis

Diagnostic procedures available (e.g., computed tomography
scan, laboratory studies, psychological testing)

Diagnostic observation by trained staff

Treatment

Medical management of severely disturbed psychiatric clients

Therapeutic monitoring of clients receiving electroconvulsive
therapy or withdrawing from drugs or alcohol, medication
initiation in fragile clients, and forced compliance with
treatment

Therapeutic containment of disturbed clients

Therapeutic milieu with multiple modalities for care

By emphasizing the resources of an inpatient setting, the clinician
need not rely exclusively on the severity of the client's diagnosis or
threats of harm to justify utilization of inpatient care. Thus, the decision to admit is based on the need to protect the client, gain access to
laboratory or diagnostic services not easily obtained in the community, and obtain benefits derived from intensive, multimodal interventions.

Outpatient care, on the other hand, offers psychiatric care of
less intensity to clients who are able to continue living without the
need for a secure environment. A variety of options for care exist:
medication maintenance; group, individual, and family therapy;
linkage with an available resource for emotional support; and a variety of social supports necessary to facilitate reentry into the community. The selection of outpatient facilities for continued care is based
on the client's ability to engage in psychotherapy, a desire for that
form of care, and an ability to function safely in a setting with few
constraints. For example, involuntary treatment has been mandated
in outpatient settings with minimal regard for the setting's ability to
monitor involuntary care or the client's ability to benefit from this
form of treatment.[8]

An additional resource may be those intermediate measures
which ensure adherence, such as outreach services, visiting nurse services, and an appointment with a specified therapist. The growing
number of services in this category attests to the need for care that is
tailored to the client and rests somewhere between inpatient and outpatient care. The disposition plan is therefore a combination of client
need, based on clinical assessment and degree of risk, and selection

of settings for their particular services which are needed by the individual client.

Stages of Decision Making in the Emergency Service

Within the emergency service itself, there are several stages of decision making which guide the interventions provided. Figure 9–1 depicts the three stages of decision making during a psychiatric evaluation in the emergency room. One of the first decisions made concerns the immediacy of the client's problem. This decision occurs prior to the final assessment of the clinical problem and is best described as a *triage* decision. There are three options at the outset of the initial contact. First, the clinician may determine that the severity of the client's problem warrants immediate medical or psychiatric interventions, or that the client is able to participate in a clinical interview and begin the problem-solving process. The medical or psychiatric emergency requires *immediate* use of additional staff to protect the client (or others) from further harm. Examples include violent, dangerous behavior necessitating restraint and seclusion, or the need for medical care for drug reactions, overdose, injury, and so on. In the absence of an impending clinical crisis, the clinician may proceed with the clinical interview. Triage interventions assign priority to those clients unable to wait, unlikely to be able to control violent or self-destructive impulses, or with potential medical emergencies.

The second level of decision making focuses on assessment of the clinical problem. The clinician must determine the general type of problem (i.e., organic, situational, psychotic, or characterological) and the level of risk to the client or society. Before planning intervention strategies, the clinician may request psychiatric or medical consultation for validation or assistance with the assessment process. Consultation is advised for the inexperienced clinician to solidify clinical skills, but, more importantly, it offers *all* members of the team an opportunity to consider alternative diagnoses as well as creative disposition planning.

As the assessment process moves toward formulation of the clinical problem, the clinician begins to narrow the selection of treatment resources. Decisions about hospitalization versus outpatient care are clear in many cases. In others, consultation adds another opinion to the assessment process.

The third stage of decision making focuses on disposition planning. The choice of intervention strategy will reflect the interface between the clinical problem, the community resources, and the client's

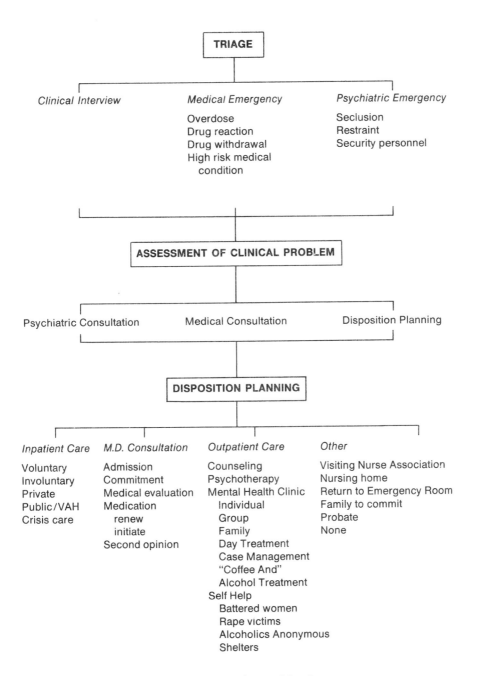

Figure 9–1 Decision-making process in psychiatric emergency care.

agenda for care. We have listed the various options which exist in most communities for psychiatric care. Choices are usually limited to inpatient care, outpatient care, and other services which represent intermediate care or nonpsychiatric services helpful in linking clients to traditional treatment settings. Other services provide safe, contained care for clients with special needs, such as the elderly or victims of abuse.

Balancing Clinical Data

The choice of disposition plan will depend on the balance of factors in each clinical situation. The severity of the clinical problem and the risk of suicidal or homicidal behavior are offset by the resources of the client and the community, the amount of support available to the client, and the likelihood of adherence to the designated plan. A model of these factors is presented in Figure 9–2. Using the restrictiveness of the treatment setting as a guide for determining intervention strategies, the factors are placed on a teeter-totter balance to display the direction of the interventions. The severity of the client's clinical problem is dependent on the seriousness of the diagnosis, the apparent symptoms, and the degree of impaired reality contact and impulse control. An additional factor is the presence of suicidal or homicidal ideation/threat/intent, which adds to the seriousness of the problem. These two factors are placed on one side of the scale, but may be separated to determine overall seriousness. For example, psychotic symptoms such as hallucinations, delusions, or depersonalization, may not be accompanied by a serious suicidal or homicidal risk. Therefore, these two components would occupy separate places on the severity continuum of the scale.

The other side of the scale is reserved for *resources* for care (e.g. financial, transportation, third-party reimbursement); *support* from family, professional services, and other persons in the client's social network who are available and interested in returning the client to

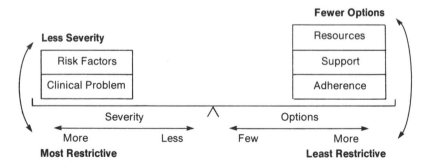

Figure 9–2   Balance of factors in disposition planning.

health; and the likelihood of *adherence* to the prescribed plan (e.g., the client's agenda, preferences for care). The continuum for this side of the scale represents multiple versus few resources and options. The scale is balanced by the number of options which are likely to allow the client to receive care in the least restrictive setting. Again, each of the three factors on this side of the scale can be measured separately and can occupy various positions on the continuum. For example, the client who has access to resources and supportive individuals, but is unlikely to agree with a treatment plan, may not be allowed voluntary care unless the severity of the symptoms and risks are minimal.

Figures 9–3 and 9–4 are examples of extreme variations in the configuration of clinical data. Figure 9–3 represents the most severe risk and symptomatology requiring treatment in the securest/most restrictive environment. Without ample resources or adherence to the treatment plan, clients lose disposition options as the severity of their symptoms increases. Maximal options and minimal severity of symptoms are noted in Figure 9–4. This would result in treatment in the least restrictive environment of the client's choice.

Conceptual Model of Decision-Making

The model developed by Runyan offers a practical framework of intervention reasoning.[9] He identifies three major components to his framework.

1. Scientific-empirical reasoning, which includes the more traditional activities of assessment, diagnosis, and prediction
2. Technical-economic reasoning, which involves the most useful range of techniques and strategies that might be employed in a given situation

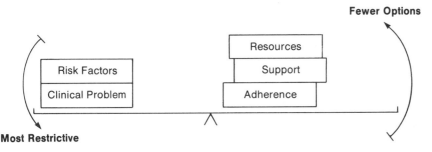

Figure 9–3   Serious clinical problem with high risk and few resources/ options for care.

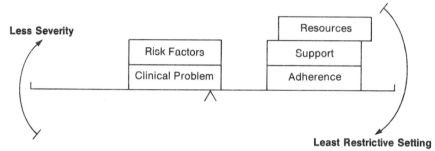

Figure 9-4 Multiple resources/options for treatment of a less serious clinical problem.

3. Valuative-ethical reasoning, which involves the range of interests and concerns of related systems

Given the complexity of clinical decision making and the position it occupies between art and science, this model offers some reference points for the *process* of evaluating clinical data. To a large extent, these components are complementary during assessment and intervention activities, enriching the clinician's judgment. Only rarely does the decision-making process in the psychiatric emergency service rely exclusively on one component.

Scientific-empirical reasoning refers to the mix of scientific principles and experiential reasoning common to clinical practice. Psychiatric care has long relied on empirical decisions in the absence of standardized objective criteria by which to diagnose clinical symptoms. The scientific base has been expanding in recent years with the DSM III criteria for diagnosis, resulting in more precise somatic interventions with pharmacotherapy, electroconvulsive therapy, and diagnostic examinations.

This same precision is only now emerging in psychiatric emergency care. The time constraints, severity of the illness, and complexity of intervention strategies have undoubtedly delayed the development of scientific principles which guide clinical practice in this treatment arena. Nonetheless, it is useful to apply the existing standards of diagnostic and risk assessment to the emergency service.

One approach is the use of a dichotomous scale (yes versus no) for each of the stages of assessment.

Our experience indicates that it is useful for the clinician consciously to think through this "yes versus no" response to each of the above categories, recognizing that action in the form of intervention and treatment is contingent upon this thinking. For example, the clinician must determine the likelihood of dangerous behavior in a client even though the data base may not be sufficient to make a decision

	Yes	No
Diagnosis		
Situational		
Personality disorder		
Psychosis		
Organic		
Risk factors		
Suicidal		
Homicidal		
Treatment options		
Support		
Resources		
Adherence to plan		

with absolute assurance. Although the data base or the methods of assessment are not precise enough to predict outcomes accurately, the clinician is forced to make the best decision and devise intervention strategies.

With increased clinical experience and scientific principles to guide clinical learning, the clinician becomes more confident in relying on the mixture of art and science. The decision-making model of the text merely defines the parameters of safe clinical practice. These guideposts signal the clinician's attention to commonly occurring phenomena in psychiatric emergency care. Thus, the hypotheses that are developed regarding diagnosis, risk, and resources for care prevent early closure on assessment or intervention planning.

A central issue in considering intervention plans is the restrictiveness of the treatment options. The term *restrictiveness* denotes the constraints placed on the client's freedom in receiving psychiatric care. The most restrictive form of treatment is involuntary, usually in an inpatient setting. Involuntary care has also been mandated in outpatient settings, allowing more freedom on a day-to-day basis but nonetheless involuntarily prescribed.[10] Hospitalization represents more restrictive care than outpatient care or day treatment.

As the factors of risk, diagnosis, and resources become clearly assessed in the interview, the rationale for interventions begins to emerge. The clinician determines the needs of the client as they interface with the resources of settings. Inpatient settings, however, provide more than safety for clients, and outpatient clinics may be sufficient settings for the delivery of care to chronically psychotic clients. Safety needs are best met in the inpatient setting, but community resources may be sufficient to maintain clients when this setting is not available.

The scientific portion of the assessment process relies on the standard frameworks for assessment described in Chapter 2. The psychiatric history, the MSE, and the clinical interview process have been refined over the years to include the most pertinent areas for examination. Similarly, the suicide scales listed in Chapter 4 have been well researched and their predictive value improved. Dangerousness remains an elusive quality in emergency assessment, but nonetheless an important aspect of decision making. The criteria for diagnosis (as presented in DSM III) offer the clinician constellations of signs and symptoms which foster improved interrater reliability.

The empirical reasoning portion of clinical judgment is derived from past clinical and life experiences which have been blended with the scientific principles of psychiatric care. Given the uniqueness of each case, empirical reasoning improves the predictive quality of the clinician's decision making. For example, the clinician is able to predict which configurations of signs and symptoms are likely to result in poor compliance or aggressive behavior. It is this predictive quality that often shifts the intervention toward more or less restrictive treatment settings in the absence of other criteria by which to make this decision.

Technical reasoning adds a different dimension to disposition planning. As noted earlier, the resources of inpatient settings described by Friedman[11] direct the clinician's attention toward those settings. The variability between settings becomes an added factor in the choice of a specific inpatient setting. Not only the programmatic differences but also the eligibility requirements of settings impinge on decision making. Veterans' Hospitals have the most restrictive eligibility requirements (veteran status from the armed services); state hospitals have lesser requirements usually related to catchment area and income.

Programmatic differences generally refer to the emphases of the setting, the length of stay, and the philosophy of the treatment team. Knowledge of these factors allows the clinician to match the client's needs more closely with the setting's resources. Thus, clients who require only brief treatment or a diagnostic evaluation are best referred to short-term settings which provide these types of care. Drug and alcohol problems are usually treated in programs which specialize in those disorders. Long-term facilities offer more modalities for care of the client who has severe, incapacitating symptoms that have not responded to briefer treatment methods.

The choices of treatment settings depicted in Figure 9–1 offer a framework of community options. The specific programs, eligibility requirements, and cost/benefit ratios of each setting are only some of the data clinicians must be familiar with prior to arranging a referral. This maximizes the benefits of the referral for the client and avoids obvious referral failures secondary to inadequate program capability (e.g., inability to care for violent clients).

Once the clinician has learned the repertoire of community agencies and their respective treatment interests and capabilities, the decision-making process can effectively utilize the technical aspects of intervention planning.

Figure 9–2 offers one model by which the critical elements of the assessment process are weighed. Severity of symptoms and risk factors are balanced by the options and resources for care and the client's willingness to participate in the treatment program. The most disturbed clients with the greatest degree of risk require multiple options and resources in order to receive care in the *least* restrictive setting. This decision would be based on empirical reasoning which provided a certain degree of safety for the client. A less disturbed client might utilize the inpatient setting for its diagnostic capability or specialized treatment program, making this a decision based on technical reasoning.

The *valuative-ethical* reasoning in Runyan's model refers to the concerns of the entire system in generating a treatment strategy. This includes the client, clinician, family/support network, community, and referral settings. The interests of each member or system are integrated into the final decision on further treatment options. This level of decision making is probably most arbitrary, since there are numerous options for care and only minimal criteria by which to choose among them. Thus, the clinician must be cognizant of his or her own value system, that of the client and support network, and that of the community.

Delivery of care and development of publicly supported programs vary widely. Rural areas are apt to be less tolerant of certain psychological problems at the outset, but once the client's behavior becomes predictable, community tolerance may become quite high. Metropolitan areas often have multiple resources for care, and the population density allows the severely chronically mentally ill to be less conspicuous.

The decisions that arise from a valuative-ethical base may seem the most arbitrary. Restrictive criteria for involuntary care will mandate the release of an individual in one city but not in another with less restrictive statutes. Inpatient settings may refuse clients on the basis of previous poor compliance in the program or the mix of currently admitted clients, which prevents them from taking a client with a particular problem. Funding cutbacks may force the elimination of programs, thus depriving clients of specialized services. These influences on the decision-making process are probably the most frustrating to clinicians as they attempt to act as advocates for clients and link them with effective treatment settings. Nonetheless, these are the typical experiences faced by clinicians who work at the interface of systems and must negotiate the pathway into care for clients.

Clinical Application

We will present some clinical examples from the emergency service and evaluate the data according to the figures presented in this chapter. Additionally, we will use the dichotomous scale to demonstrate the problem-solving process that directs the intervention planning.

Clinical Example 9–1

The client is a 32-year-old white separated male brought to the emergency service by the police. They were summoned by his wife after the client came to her house. When she refused to speak with him, he removed his clothing and poured purple paint over his body. On examination the client is cooperative, speaks rapidly, and has a very intense manner. He denies having any emotional problems, stating that the police should not have brought him to the emergency service. He and his wife have been separated for a year, and he now realizes that this was a mistake and wishes to return to her. She has refused any contact with him, so today he decided to paint himself purple (his wife's favorite color) so that she would find him irresistible and return to him. He refuses to acknowledge that it was his wife who called the police, and he has no plans other than to stay in town until he is reunited with his wife.

Using the stages of decision making (Figure 9–1), this client would be considered a psychiatric emergency at the outset of the interview. It was necessary to have him washed before the paint became more difficult to remove, and to have the police remain with him during the interview. In his absence of insight into his problem, he was considered to be at risk for unpredictable behavior, although he had not been violent up to this point.

The findings on the dichotomous scale for determining the severity of his problem, risk factors, resources/options, and adherence are as follows:

	Yes	No
Diagnosis		
Situational		X
Personality disorder	?	
Psychosis	X	
Organic	?	
Risk factors		
Suicidal		X
Homicidal	?	
Treatment options		
Support		X
Resources	?	
Adherence to plan		X

According to the data available in the interview and from the police, the most likely diagnosis to consider *at this point* would be a psychotic disorder, as evidenced by the client's illogical reasoning and his behavior. There is no way of determining at this time if he also has a personality disorder or an organic condition with subclinical features. He is not presently suicidal, although his risk of dangerous behavior is high secondary to his intention to return to his wife in the face of her refusal to take him back. His attempts to gain her attention may escalate with repeated rejections by her.

His options for care are less well known, although he may have access to insurance or qualify for involuntary care in a nearby institution. His support system is minimal and is unlikely to have the resources to care for him in his current agitated state. His adherence is markedly low in the face of poor insight, impaired judgment, and the single-minded goal of returning to his wife.

The balance of these factors (Figure 9–5) would lean toward treatment in a restrictive setting, probably against his will. The advantages of this plan provide safety, protection of the client (and his wife), a diagnostic evaluation, and forced compliance with therapeutic measures.

Clinical Example 9–2

The client is a 25-year-old black single mother of two. She presents to the emergency service for help with her depression. She has been feeling sad for several months, with loss of appetite, insomnia (difficulty falling asleep), and fatigue. She is not sure what has caused her to feel bad, but would like help. She denies having any suicidal ideation and has never had psychiatric care before. As the interview progresses, she shows evidence of paranoid thinking without a formalized delusional system. She has few friends, does not socialize, and has lost contact with her family. Her main sources of financial support are welfare and child assistance. She denies having hallucinations or delusions but is afraid something might happen to her children. Her ability to care for the children has not been compromised by her emotional state. Her affect is flat throughout much of the interview, and she is relatively detached from the interview process. There is no stated preference for care, except that she refuses medication and admission to the hospital or an outpatient appointment.

From the interview, the extent of this woman's problem is unclear. Her complaints of depression are difficult to assess on the basis of neurovegetative findings (i.e., no weight loss, difficulty in falling asleep, and fatigue). She is not suicidal, but appears somewhat paranoid in some of her statements. This response may be related to her inability to trust the interviewer, however. Her life situation is obviously lacking in support and resources for care. Lastly, she has no plans for future psychiatric care, but seems truly in need of some assistance.

Using the dichotomous scale to evaluate the data base, one might conclude that she has a personality disorder or an impending psychotic process. Her situational context is unsatisfying to her but has not changed recently. There is no evidence of suicidal and homi-

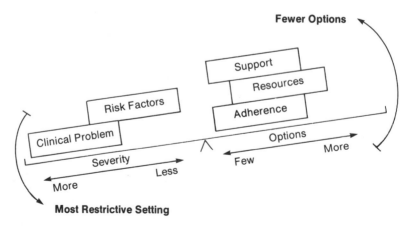

Figure 9–5   Clinical example 9–1: Balance of factors.

cidal tendencies, but her ability to care for her children may decline if the situation worsens. Here adherence to a plan seems low in the face of her disinterest in most of the traditional options for psychiatric care.

	Yes	No
Diagnosis		
Situational		X
Personality disorder	?	
Psychosis	?	
Organic		X
Risk factors		
Suicidal		X
Homicidal		X
Treatment options		
Support		X
Resources		X
Adherence to plan		X

The balance of these factors (Figure 9–6) would lean slightly toward a serious problem, with few resources to assist with interventions. This would result in the use of less traditional resources provided by public assistance programs. Our concern for this client's emotional state and that of her children resulted in a referral to the visiting nurse agency in her catchment area. Agency staff were instructed to make a home visit, evaluate the situation, and attempt to link her with the local mental health clinic. This resource had ongoing consultation with the mental health clinic, which ensured better attention to the emotional problems this woman might have been experiencing and provided a resource to monitor the safety and welfare of her children. The client was very agreeable to this plan, probably because the nurse would visit her at home.

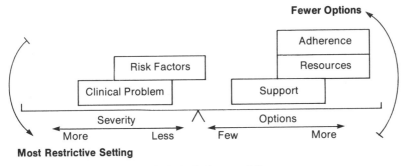

Figure 9–6   Clinical example 9–2: Balance of factors.

Summary

The decision-making process employed in the psychiatric emergency service is a crucial part of the clinician's role. The development of disposition plans based on a *complete* clinical data base is rare. Instead, the clinician must rely on a mixture of clinical data, previous experience with clients, and principles of psychiatric emergency care. The hypotheses that guide the assessment of the clinical problem narrow the interview process toward the most likely explanations for the immediate problem.

Next, the clinician must determine the risk factors likely to affect the type of setting necessary for *safe* care. When the likelihood of dangerous behavior (suicidal or homicidal) is great, the clinician must utilize restrictive settings for the protection of the client and/or society.

The client's clinical problem and risk for harm are only two of the elements of the decision-making process. The availability of resources and adherence to the treatment plan create situations in which less restrictive alternative treatment plans can be implemented.

The models and diagrams presented in this chapter are designed to help the clinician evaluate data from various vantage points. Organization of clinical data and a framework for determining the reliability of data provide a foundation on which to base clinical judgment.

References

1. Khuri, R., and Wood, K.: The role of diagnosis in a psychiatric emergency setting. *Hospital and Community Psychiatry, 35,* 715–718, 1984.

2. Babiker, J. E.: Determinants of outcome in a psychiatric emergency clinic. *Scottish Medical Journal, 19,* 196–199, 1974.

3. Comstock, B. S.: Psychiatric emergency intensive care. *Psychiatric Clinics of North America, 6,* 305–316, 1983.

4. Friedman, S.; Margolis, R.; David, O.; and Kesselman, M.: Predicting psychiatric admission from an emergency room. Psychiatric, psychosocial, and methodological factors. *The Journal of Nervous and Mental Disease, 171,* 155–158, 1983.

5. Friedman, R. S.: Hospital treatment of psychiatric emergencies. *Psychiatric Clinics of North America, 6,* 293–303, 1983.

6. Ibid.

7. Ibid.

8. Miller, R. D., and Fiddleman, P. B.: Outpatient commitment: Treatment in the least restrictive environment? *Hospital and Community Psychiatry, 35,* 147–151, 1984.

9. Runyan, W. M.: How should treatment recommendations be made? Three studies of the logical and empirical base of clinical decision-making. *Journal of Clinical and Consulting Psychology, 45,* 552–558, 1977.

10. Miller and Fiddleman, op. cit.

11. Friedman, op. cit.

PSYCHIATRIC EMERGENCY CARE MODELS

The 1970s produced rapid growth in the understanding and definition of psychiatric emergency care. Studies clearly delineated the populations served by emergency services and the types of interventions provided. As noted in Chapter 1, early emphases were placed on assessment, evaluation, disposition planning, and interagency working relationships to accommodate the needs of clients.

During this process, the concept of the psychiatric emergency began to be defined. McPherson has cited the American Psychiatric Association's draft version definition of a mental health emergency: "an acute disturbance of thought, mood, behavior or social relationship that requires an immediate intervention as defined by the patient, family, or community."[1] The interventions used in these emergency situations are the next area of investigation, since they clearly exist outside inpatient or outpatient service settings.

The growth of these new service models can be directly traced to the limitations of existing services for psychiatric emergencies. Emergency service clinicians have documented the poor compliance rates of clients, as reflected in appointments to outpatient clinics, and have noted the unavailability of inpatient beds for clients requiring admission. Additionally, many clients did not require all of the services provided in these settings, which precluded their acceptance as referrals or their willingness to seek care.

In response to this situation, clinicians began to develop their own resources for clients discharged from the emergency service. These will be described in the next section. It is important to remember, however, that these services originated in client demands for easily accessible mental health services and community demands for a resource to be used by the police, family members, and other health care agencies faced with an emergency situation.

In this chapter, we will review the origin of psychiatric emergency care models and their functional capacities today. The future of these programs will also be addressed in light of current research efforts and changing mental health policies, which affect funding resources.

Service Delivery Models

As the emergency room of the general hospital became an alternative "family physician" for immediate medical care, the psychiatric population soon acted on a similar request for emergency mental health services. Clients arrived for care at the insistence of concerned family members or the police, or on their own initiative. As with the medical population, many of these clients' problems were considered less than urgent, but nonetheless required some type of care. Emergency

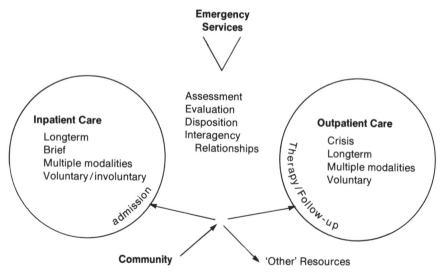

Figure 10–1   Early model of psychiatric emergency services.

services responded by providing psychiatric clinicians to evaluate and care for this growing population.

Figure 10–1 depicts the original relationship of the psychiatric emergency service to inpatient and outpatient settings, as well as the community at large. Emergency care services provided included assessment, evaluation, disposition planning, and interagency working relationships. Care focused primarily on evaluating clients and routing them to traditional treatment settings for further treatment. Psychiatric needs requiring other forms of care went unmet.

In order to expand the care for these clients, additional services evolved. Figure 10–2 lists these services and the complex community-emergency service relationships which followed. *Emergency intensive care* or emergency stabilization has developed for those clients who should be treated in a more intensive environment than that of traditional inpatient care.[2] This has reduced the length of stay and prevented hospitalization in long-term care settings. Overlapping with outpatient services are *return visits* to the emergency service for clients able to work on their problems but not in need of formal outpatient psychotherapy. *Outreach care* has brought mental health services to the client's home or the nonpsychiatric agency.

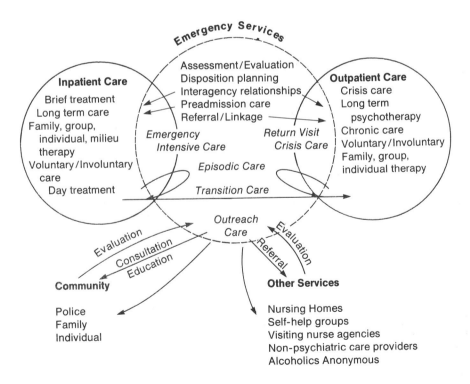

Figure 10–2 Actual and potential emergency service models.

An additional form of treatment, *episodic care,* is available to clients in treatment elsewhere who are in crisis situations and need additional immediate services. This brief intervention is somewhat preventive in that clients are linked back to traditional settings before the crisis reaches threatening proportions.

Transition care is another potential service under the rubric of emergency services. Here clients could be followed as they move from inpatient to outpatient settings when the linkage mechanisms are weak. The referral coordinator model discussed in Chapter 9 is one method of linking clients with outpatient settings prior to discharge. This may not always be possible, particularly when clients are discharged to communities far from the inpatient facility. Staff could contact clients, ensure their arrival at the facility, and integrate the social network members into the care plan.

The development of these emergency intervention strategies has broadened the scope of emergency care. More aspects of the crisis/emergency situation can now be handled by emergency services. The use of rapid tranquilization and the work with support networks have proved effective in returning severely disturbed clients to their homes in a few days.[3] Return visits offer clients an opportunity to resolve immediate problems in only a few sessions with familiar staff.

Community Response

Although some emergency problems have been resolved, there is a continued need to deal with alternative care settings. Understanding the courses of psychiatric disorders allows the clinician to determine the best setting for continued care. Similarly, the selection of non-psychiatric outpatient settings individualizes care for clients who do not require the special care of the mental health clinic. By increasing the treatment network for clients with psychiatric emergencies, greater responsibility is shifted to these new programs. Nursing homes, shelters for battered women and rape victims, visiting nurse agencies, and others are now able to care for more disturbed individuals with the assistance of emergency service personnel.

The increase in community responsibility has created opportunities for consultation with and education of community agency personnel. Workshops and manuals have been developed for emergency medical technicians, police, group home operators, landlords, and nursing agency personnel to prepare them to deal with psychiatric emergency situations.[4] Training of these individuals depends on understanding the differences between inpatient, outpatient, and emergency care. The interventions used during an emergency situation are not necessarily the same as those applied to inpatient or outpatient care settings.

Expanding on the crisis intervention model, emergency care is characterized by increased action by the clinician and more direction in designing interventions.[5,6] McCarthy has noted the use of confrontation, reassurance, stabilization and resolution, and maximal resource integration as common therapeutic strategies for emergency care.[7] Unlike outpatient therapy, which may be more passive, the emergency situation requires direction and advice to facilitate psychological stabilization.

The use of selected therapeutic approaches has set emergency care apart from traditional forms of psychiatry. Unlike crisis intervention techniques which are designed primarily for functional individuals, emergency psychiatric treatment covers a broad spectrum of psychiatric disorders, which are often extreme in form. As more is learned about the value of these techniques, community personnel can adopt them to control severely disturbed individuals in community settings.

Special Populations

As the modalities for emergency care become differentiated from traditional therapies, greater attention can be given to the needs of special populations. The elderly, children, alcoholics, violent individuals, and victims of abuse require different evaluation methods and intervention strategies. The development of strategies for these populations was delayed until the foundation of emergency care was identified. Each of these populations will now be discussed, with a brief mention of their diagnostic and treatment problems.

The elderly client has somewhat special psychological problems, in addition to the limitations associated with the assessment process.[8] Hearing, speech, and ambulation problems are likely to slow down the evaluation and require alternative assessment methods. The search for organic mental disorders and contributing age-appropriate medical problems also precludes a strict psychiatric interpretation of emotional symptoms. Almost more importantly, the elderly clients today resist psychiatric care because of long-standing concerns about being labeled mental patients and stigmatized by this form of treatment. Case finding becomes a primary issue in dealing with these clients, who otherwise would receive less than adequate psychiatric care.

The pediatric client also needs separate evaluation procedures. The use of MSE techniques, and attention to family issues and developmental difficulties, differ from the approaches used with the adult population.[9] Both younger and older clients are high-risk candidates for suicide, and therefore alert the clinician to age-specific mental health care issues. The pediatric population is also more likely to require family interventions, since the family is a common source of the emotional difficulty or the network most likely to facilitate recovery. School-related issues are the next most common source of interpersonal problems.

More recently, attention has focused on the alcoholic client in the emergency service. Previously, these clients fell somewhere between psychiatry and medicine. They were difficult to assess when intoxicated, yet their impending medical emergencies prevented their discharge to the community. Too often, little effort was made to persuade them to seek psychiatric care for alcoholism or even brief detoxification. Whitney has described the benefits of an organized alcohol team which provides initial assessment, coordination of care with medical staff, and referral to treatment or detoxification programs.[10] These interventions have been useful in mobilizing family systems and acknowledging the need for alcohol-related treatment of previously neglected populations. With the increasing numbers of special programs for drug and alcohol abuse, the emergency service clinician is better prepared to intervene, rather than labeling these clients as hopeless or unmotivated.

Lastly, the victims of abuse are less stigmatized by psychiatric interventions that prepare clients to cope with the predictable stages of victimization, rather than addressing the emotional upheaval of being victimized. These clients require emotional support, but this is perhaps best provided in environments that offer shelter, self-help, and access to child care and legal information. In this way, the multiple ramifications of the violent episode can be addressed in one setting.

The growing emphasis on the needs of special populations promises to define emergency care more systematically. As previously noted, the fundamentals of assessment and the intervention strategies of the emergency service have now been defined. The emphasis on selected *groups* of clients (and clinical problems) has the potential to move this field toward an integrated care model that is only partially dependent on diagnostic classifications. Regardless of the clinical diagnosis, care is planned according to individual needs, community resources, support network availability, and subspecialty practices (e.g., alcohol treatment, geropsychiatry). Similarly, the need for immediately available services has produced new programs not previously considered feasible in the treatment of psychiatric disorders (e.g., emergency intensive care, outpatient management of psychotic clients, and home visits). With the addition of these alternative treatment strategies, the influence of emergency psychiatric care is now being felt throughout the field of medicine.

Future Research

With the increased sophistication of psychiatric emergency care, avenues for research have expanded. Early studies documented the assessment needs of various emergency services and the types of interventions employed or needed to care for these populations. These reports have clarified the clinical concepts of care, making room for more formal investigations.

Slaby and McPherson have listed several aspects of emergency psychiatric care in need of further research.[11,12] The following list is adapted from their recommendations:

1. Improve diagnostic accuracy.
2. Monitor changing utilization patterns over time.
3. Determine cost-effective methods of delivering emergency care.
4. Define the most effective types of care for selected clinical problems and/or populations.
5. Study the diagnostic reliability of emergency decision making.
6. Develop quality assurance measures of assessment and referral mechanisms.
7. Follow up clients released from the emergency service to assess their satisfaction and progress secondary to interventions.
8. Define biological markers or objective methods of measuring psychological dysfunctions.
9. Study the milieu of the emergency service and its effect on the delivery of care and on staff morale.

These research endeavors reinforce the growth of the emergency psychiatric field. Testing various treatment approaches, understanding the effect of emergency care on the client, and searching for more refined diagnostic methods will lend further credibility to this type of care. Although the deterrents to research in emergency services are great, Slaby remains optimistic that these can be overcome.[13] He believes that "clinical case study methods" provide one way of following specific types of clients over time to identify their response to interventions.

In addition to research opportunities, emergency service personnel training has come under better control. Psychiatrists have organized approaches for residents-in-training which lessen the burden of providing care in isolation. Structured learning environments have evolved to include supervisory rounds, case conferences, and presentation of psychiatric emergency care principles.[14]

Funding Issues

The 1980s have brought radical changes to health care through the diagnostic-related groups and prospective payment methods. These cost-containment approaches of third-party reimbursement are already beginning to change the delivery of health care. Although psychiatric care has not developed universally accepted standards for its practice, this will occur in the very near future.

Psychiatric emergency services will fare either extremely well or extremely poorly with these revised payment plans. On the favorable side, emergency services have reduced inpatient stays and returned clients quickly to the community. They have also intervened with severely disabled clients on an outpatient basis, possibly preventing unnecessary use of inpatient services. On the other side, these services are located in emergency rooms, which are usually reserved for only critically ill clients, thus driving up their cost. The clinical problems cover the entire diagnostic spectrum, making it almost impossible to differentiate emergency from non-emergency therapy cases.

In order to justify the existence of these programs, their comparative value must be defined. This places emergency care in the position of competing with existing services in order to justify cost-effective methods of treatment. Will psychiatric emergency care be more cost effective than inpatient treatment? Will pressure be placed on these programs to utilize existing services which are already funded for similar purposes?

Financial constraints are likely to curtail many of the recent developments in psychiatric emergency care unless these programs become recognized, viable alternative treatment methods. Some of these services may shift to alternative sites if psychiatry follows the direction of medical care. Primary care settings (which are already handling many psychiatric disorders), urgent-visit clinics, and storefront neighborhood health centers may prove useful models for emergency mental health services. If the attraction of emergency care is related to its accessibility and anonymity, the emergency room location may be less important. At any rate, the value of emergency services has been well established over the last twenty years, and client demand for them clearly remains high.

The Contribution of Nursing

Clinical specialists have become visible members of the psychiatric emergency service. Their contributions include assessment, evaluation, discharge planning, direct care, and management of the emergency service. The nurse with advanced preparation is uniquely suited to this setting. Unlike other mental health professionals who are psychiatrically prepared but not grounded in medical health care, the nurse brings a balanced perspective to the care of these clients. The public health perspective, medical experience, and psychiatric nursing expertise are necesary elements of emergency psychiatric care.

The mixture of organic causes of psychiatric symptoms, and the need for creative disposition plans and sound therapeutic approaches, creates an exciting area of practice. The organization of this book has focused on these issues, with the underlying assumption that the role of nursing should not only continue, but expand. The increased interest of psychiatrists in psychiatric emergency services indicates a growing desire to manage these services. This creates further opportunities for interdisciplinary practice in an area previously avoided.

References

1. McPherson, D. E.: Teaching and research in emergency psychiatry. *Canadian Journal of Psychiatry, 29,* 50–54, 1984.
2. Comstock, B. S.: Psychiatric emergency intensive care. *Psychiatric Clinics of North America, 6,* 305–316, 1983.
3. Ibid.
4. McPherson, op. cit.

5. Fauman, B. J.: Psychiatric residency training in the management of emergencies. *Psychiatric Clinics of North America, 6,* 325–334, 1983.

6. McCarthy, E. A.: Resolution of the psychiatric emergency in the emergency department. *Psychiatric Clinics of North America, 6,* 281–292, 1983.

7. Ibid.

8. Herst, L. D.: Emergency psychiatry for the elderly. *Psychiatric Clinics of North America, 6,* 271–280, 1983.

9. Turgay, A.: Psychiatric emergencies in children. *Psychiatric Journal of the University of Ottawa, 7,* 254–260, 1982.

10. Whitney, R. B.: Alcoholics in emergency rooms. *Bulletin of the New York Academy of Medicine, 59,* 216–221, 1983.

11. Slaby, A. E.: Research strategies in emergency psychiatry. *Psychiatric Clinics of North America, 6,* 347–360, 1983.

12. McPherson, op. cit.

13. Slaby, op. cit.

14. Fauman, op. cit.

INDEX

A

Abstract reasoning, 25
  diagnostic data, 72, 73f
Abstraction ability, testing, 34 – 35
Abuse, reporting, 118
Abuse victims, 108, 117, 123
  assessment, 118 – 19
  characteristics, 117 – 18
  safety, 118
  special procedures, 211
Access
  restrictions, 146
Access barriers, 150 – 51, 157,
    158
  reduction, 151
Access variable, 145 – 46, 150
Acting-out behavior, 57
Activity, diminished, 32
  observation, 32
Adaptation, poor, 36
Adaptive style, characterological
    problem, 57

Adherence, 12, 129, 130, 179, 186, 193
  conflicts, 165
  defined, 163, 164
  factors, 175, 175t, 176t
  interaction model, 167 – 72
  negotiation, 167, 168, 180
  philosophy, 163
  relationship to demoralization, 167
  services improving, 174 – 76
Adjustment
  expected degree, 51
  patterns, 76
Admissions to inpatient setting,
    diagnostic categories, 187, 187t
Adolescent client, suicidal behavior,
    100
Affect, examination of, 24
Affective disorders, 54, 56, 62
  depression, 61 – 63
  mania, 60 – 61
Affective state, evaluation, 28, 31
Age of client, 26, 28
  psychotic diagnosis, compliance, 167